Anna-Marie W.

Amanda's FATHER

by

Martha Denlinger Stahl

Amanda's Father

by Martha Denlinger Stahl

Library of Congress Number: 2010916700
International Standard Book Number: 978-1-60126-261-5

Published 2010 by

Masthof Press

219 Mill Road

Morgantown, PA 19543-9516

PROLOGUE

The ringing of the telephone awakened me from a sound sleep. Turning on the light, I struggled out of bed and shuffled across the room. “Hello?”

“Amanda.” My 93-year-old father’s voice from his room in the nursing home boomed out at me.

“Papa, you woke me up. It’s 12:30! Are you all right?”

“Oh, I’m okay. I just saw this phone here and pressed the button and I got you.”

Why had I programmed in my number?

“I’d rather talk to you in the morning, Papa. You’d better go back to bed.”

“I’m going to get dressed and go out for breakfast.”

“No, Papa, don’t do that. It’s the middle of the night. It’s time to sleep.”

“Oh, I see. It *is* 12:30. Well, I’m going for breakfast now, and talk to you later. Good-bye.”

After I hung up the phone, my thoughts kept me awake for hours. I'd worked hard to find good nursing care for Papa and had entered him in a nearby retirement home a few weeks earlier. I lay there planning how to keep this night calling from happening again. *I'll tell the nurse to disconnect his phone from 10 p.m. to 7 a.m.,*

Sleep still evaded me. I couldn't keep my thoughts from the story of my life with Papa. Papa now lived close by and called me in the middle of the night when I would rather not hear from him. I remembered so many times when my brother and sisters and I longed for him to call or come home. With mixed emotions I recalled the long separations, suspense, anger, and tears, and how even through it all I'd loved Papa and had always been glad to see him.

CHAPTER 1

"Papa, Papa, do come."

"Papa, Papa, do come," Andy and I chanted as we both stood vigil at the front window. It was one of many nights when we waited eagerly for Papa, but once again we sat down to supper without him.

The next evening we had already eaten supper when I heard the familiar hum of the nearly new 1940 Pontiac interrupting our after-supper routine. Papa sold cars, so as a salesman he got to drive lots of different cars.

"Papa's here," called Andy as we all rushed out onto the porch with a jubilant welcome.

Mother, dressed in a Mennonite-style cape faded print dress, with a slightly soiled blue checkered apron, her black hair pinned back neatly under her white bonnet-shaped head covering, greeted Papa with a weak smile. Her appearance contrasted our Papa with his light brown hair and blue eyes, dressed in a white shirt, dark blue pin striped business suit and a matching long tie.

Mother asked, “Where *were* you, Steve?”

“Well, Mary, I had to show a new Pontiac to a man who works until 6 p.m. Am I ever hungry!”

Mother, as always, accepted his explanation, and proceeded to set out the warmed-up mashed potatoes, sausage, and green beans. If she doubted his words, she didn’t let us see that.

• • • • •

We all gathered around as Papa ate. Papa looked at me and asked, “Where did you get those yellow ribbons, Amanda? You look so pretty with your hair braided like that.”

I smiled. Papa could always say something to make me feel good.

“Did you have a good day in school?”

“Sure,” I continued, “and guess what! We had a fruit roll. You know, one of the boys slapped the ruler down on his desk, making a loud crack. That was our signal to roll the fruit up the aisles to our teacher. But our teacher bristled and got all red in the face. She had apparently never heard of such a thing.”

“‘You may all just come right up here and get your fruit. You probably needed this for your lunch,’” she scolded. “My heart pounded. Everyone was scared. We all walked meekly to the front of the room and found our own piece of fruit."

"At recess she must have talked with other teachers and learned that pupils do fruit rolls to show the teacher they *like* her. Anyway, she came into the room smiling, and apologized. 'I'm sorry,' she said. 'You may bring the fruit back and place it in this basket. And thank you, thank you! It is so kind of you.' I breathed a sigh of relief as I walked quietly up to the front and placed my apple in her basket. Others gave oranges, pears, and even bananas."

Papa grinned appreciatively, and I knew he liked my story. Then he turned to my brother.

Andy, age ten, shared his newest "invention" with Papa; and Beth, age twelve, showed her "A+" school paper. It was always fun to show things to Papa. Soon we all got busy doing dishes and then homework. Sarah, age six, played with her paper dolls and Mother took 18-month old Nan to bed. Nan didn't pay much attention to Papa; he was almost a stranger to her.

• • • • •

Papa's hours became more and more irregular. He quit the car salesman job and got a job at a commercial saw company. This work involved travel to other states. He stayed away more nights than he came home. One evening when he came home, well-dressed as usual, Mother pleaded with him, "I need to pay the rent, and the children need shoes."

"Mary, I don't have it today," he said turning away. "I should be getting a bonus soon. Then I can give you more."

"Promises, promises," complained my mother.

We soon realized that with Papa working as a traveling salesman, Mother was responsible for running the household, and we depended on her.

One afternoon when we came home from school, we did not see Mama in the kitchen as usual. "Where's Mama?" I called.

"Where is she?" echoed Andy.

We called and hunted anxiously.

Then we saw her out among the rows, pulling sweet corn for supper.

"Oh good, she's here," I said with a sigh of relief. When Mother was there, then everything was all right.

And Mother was *always* there! This gave us a strong sense of security, even in Papa's absence. Mama loved to work in the soil and everything seemed to grow for her. Fortunately, our rented property included a large garden. When Springtime arrived, Mama got busy planting peas, onions, lettuce, radishes, carrots and spinach. Later we children helped to drop beans, lima beans, and corn in nice straight rows. Lima beans grew on poles that Mama tied together like tepees. Mama always prepared tasty meals with these fresh garden veggies. When we had more than we needed for immediate use, Mama canned beans, corn, and carrots. We didn't own a freezer, but sometimes we took corn and peas to a rented frozen food locker in town.

Mama also enjoyed flowers in her garden. I liked the long row of peonies that grew along the side of the garden. Then we had grape arbors, too. And Mama canned wonderful grape juice.

And to clothe us, well, she knew how to sew, patch and mend. Of course, we all wore hand-me-downs and home made dresses. Sometimes relatives gave us things. So it was, with little money, Mama kept us well fed, properly dressed, and best of all, together.

I didn't mind hand-me-downs, although I did like colorful dresses and new shoes. I wanted to look nice like Papa. One day my teacher commented, "Amanda, you look so nice today in that orange skirt and the bright green pullover." (Both were second hand, but I didn't tell the teacher that.) I flashed my dimpled smile, as my self esteem went up a notch.

The place where our family lived was our fourth rented house since we moved off the farm when I was six years old.

Everyone had plenty of work to do, especially in the summer, and most of the time we cooperated willingly. Beth could often be found curled up with a book, and Sarah and I loved to play with paper dolls. But Mama pried us loose when she wanted our help.

World War II brought frightening experiences.

"Oh, no, not a black-out again," I groaned, as the sirens shouted their message on a dark October evening in 1941.

Our family sprang into action.

"Pull down all the blinds," ordered Mother. "Turn out the lights."

Only one small lamp in the kitchen stayed lit. As soon as we put the black drapes over the kitchen windows we all sat around the kitchen table to wait.

"May we sing?" asked Beth.

At first we didn't feel like singing.

"This is scary," said seven-year-old Sarah, trembling. "Why do we have to do this?"

"I wish Papa were here," said Andy.

"So do I," I said. "Why is Papa always away when something like this happens?" Andy, Beth, and I exchanged glances and sighed. Mother looked distressed.

In Papa's absence, Beth often tried to help us younger children feel secure. She pulled Sarah close beside her on the sofa. "It's because of war over in Germany. Just in case they'd come here and try to drop bombs, we don't want them to see where the towns and cities are."

• • • • •

"But no bombs will fall tonight, children," Mother comforted. "This is a test. Some airplanes will be flying over to see if everything is blacked out. We are all safe here now."

Still scared, we began to sing softly, "Be not dismayed what e'er betide; God will take care of you." The song calmed us and after a few songs, we could sing joyfully, "I'm so happy and here's the reason why, Jesus took my burdens all away."

After a while the sirens screamed again, signaling the end of the blackout. "Oh, good," said Andy, "I'm glad that's over."

"Me too," we girls echoed.

The songs we sang, plus the whole scary war scene, made me think seriously about my own life and the possibility of death. Knowing that I needed to make a decision to accept Jesus as my Savior, I told my mother one evening that I wanted to be a Christian.

My big sister, Beth, had already accepted Jesus and was excited about sharing her wonderful experience with me.

"Come, I'll pray with you," she said, grabbing me, and pulling me down beside her as she knelt by the bed. Beth prayed and had me pray until I felt sure my sins were forgiven and I was ready for life or death.

Both Andy and I were baptized in the Mennonite church the next spring. In preparation for baptism we went through a period of instruction and they taught us that life insurance was wrong. I, being very conscientious and the youngest in the whole class of 15 young people, stiffened and felt my ears getting hot. Finally I spoke, "What about the life insurance Papa has for us?"

The minister said, "Well, we won't hold you accountable for that. It's all right."

I breathed a sigh of relief.

Papa's church membership had earlier been discontinued by request of the minister because of his unethical financial dealings—writing bad checks. Yet on the Sundays when Papa was at home, he often took our family to church. He participated in the Sunday school class and sang the hymns heartily. Only, he did not participate in the communion service.

• • • • •

Cindy and Jody, about the ages of Sarah and me, lived four houses up the street, and we often played together. I loved playing house. We made a playhouse in the barn above the garage. Old boxes served as furniture and feed bags made curtains and table cloths. A tree stump made a fine seat, and some cracked and discolored dishes completed the setup. Occasionally we turned this into a schoolroom, and I liked to be the teacher.

One day I asked, "Whose father do you think is the most handsome?"

"My Daddy," Cindy promptly responded.

"Oh, no! My Papa is definitely the most handsome."

This argument went on for days, and I couldn't see why Cindy didn't agree with me. My Papa, tall and slender, with light brown hair and blue eyes *was* definitely the most handsome. In spite of Papa being away so much, which I did not understand, I remained loyal to him.

As time went on, Papa became more and more like a visitor, for his job as a traveling salesman with the saw company took him out of town a lot.

And then came the jolt.

Now in the 8th grade, I stayed home from school with German measles on the day when the letter came from Papa saying he was in the hospital in New Jersey, recovering from an appendectomy. I walked along with Mama to the next door neighbor's house, where Mama asked to use the telephone. We could not afford our own telephone.

I heard Mama say, “This is Mrs. Steve Johns calling. How is my husband doing since his appendectomy?” A long pause followed as Mother waited for a person to give a report.

Then I heard her say, “Why, of *course* I am. Steve Johns is my husband. How is he?” Annoyance and panic could be heard in her voice. “Oh no, it can’t be!”

Mother hung up and sat staring at the phone, shock and disbelief showing on her face.

“Mama, what’s wrong? Did Papa die?” I asked, tugging on her arm.

Mother paused again and her face got red.

“No, Amanda, he’s not dead, but the nurse says your father’s wife is there with him.”

Stunned, I had no words to respond.

CHAPTER 2

Meanwhile, as I learned later, over in New Jersey, Papa's other "wife" also got shocking news. She had just finished nursing six-month-old Julia. Holding the sleeping child brought a contented calm into her spirit as she anticipated bringing Steve home from the hospital. She was deep in pleasant thoughts when a loud knock startled her. She found two well-dressed men waiting beyond the screen door of the small row house.

"Does Steve Johns live here?" asked the heavier and older of the two men.

"He is not here, sir. He is in the hospital recovering from an appendectomy."

"Okay, but does he *live* here?"

"Why, yes, he's my husband, and these are his children." She held the now crying Julia, as two-year-old Angie held onto her skirt.

"Do you know that Steve has a wife and five children in Pennsylvania?" the stranger blurted out. Without waiting for an answer, the two men turned and left.

Stunned, trying to breathe again, Jenny looked around quickly to see if her mother had heard. Jenny couldn't tell her Catholic mother the truth—that she and Steve were not married. Steve had told her before Angie was born that he had a wife and two children, and that he could not marry her. They'd lied to Jenny's family about their marriage, but now this man said Steve had *five* children. Steve had not told *her* the truth, either.

Jenny breathed a sigh of relief when she found her mother busy in the kitchen, never questioning the knock. Jenny hoped the men would not come back to talk to Steve.

Sometimes Jenny wished she had never left the convent! She recalled the day she'd made the decision to leave. Being a nun had no longer appealed to her. She wanted to get out into the "real" world, get married, and have children.

She found a job working as a secretary for a large lumber company. Steve came in to sell a special kind of saw. She remembered noticing a sad look on the face of the handsome man, and decided to be especially nice to him and see if she could cheer him up. She even encouraged her boss to buy the saw from Steve, which pleased Steve so much that he asked to take her out to dinner.

"Steve," she had said, "why do you look so sad?"

"Sad? What makes you say that?

"I can see that you are hiding problems."

"You're perceptive, Jenny, but I really don't want to get into that. Let's just have some fun together."

They kept going out together every week or so when Steve was in the area, but Steve talked little about his personal life. She had a hard time getting to know him, but she liked dating. Then came the night when they became more involved and intimate than they had intended.

Some months later she had shocked Steve with the news, "Steve, we have to get married. I'm carrying your child."

All the color drained from his face. "Oh, Jenny, I'm sorry. I haven't told you everything. You see, I am already married and have two children in Pennsylvania."

She remembered all too well those stressful days, having no husband, and being afraid to tell her mother about the coming baby. Steve traveled a lot so she didn't see him regularly. Yet he kept coming back when his work brought him to the area.

Sometimes he wrote her letters, like the one she saved from those days of uncertainty and aloneness.

> I sure did hate to leave you today. I enjoyed being with you so much. I should be there all the time, and that's the way I want it some day, and real soon too. . . .

> I could not get my car on the boat so I am driving down. I am going to stay here in the hotel in Fredericksburg until morning. I will leave here at 6 o'clock and I can be at Williamsburg by nine where I must work all day, or maybe two days. I want to get that order. So until I see you Saturday, I am, as always, Love, Steve

Jenny recalled thinking, "He wants to be with me but he is not divorced from his wife in Pennsylvania."

She reflected on the weekend when they went off together and came back and told Jenny's family that they had gotten married. Jenny's mother liked Steve, and so accepted him, but she was angry with Jenny for not having a Catholic Church wedding.

Living with Steve and her mother and two brothers in the small house had never been easy. And now someone from Pennsylvania was on their trail, and she'd learned that he had five children instead of two.

His wife probably didn't know about Jenny and her two, either, before those men came around today. What a mess! Again she thought about life in the convent. Would her life be less complicated there? Would she be happy? But she *loved* Steve and her two precious little daughters.

• • • • •

As they slowly walked together from the hospital toward

the car, Jenny could hardly wait to tell Steve about the two men. But she didn't want to trouble him in his weakened condition.

Finally, alone in the bedroom that night, she couldn't hold it in any longer. She wanted to scream, but didn't dare with her mother and two brothers in that small house. So with calmness she didn't feel, she began slowly, "Steve, I have to tell you something."

"What's up?" Steve whispered in a tense voice.

"Two men came to the door and asked if you lived here. I told them you were in the hospital, and that yes, you are my husband. They saw our two daughters …"

"Who were they? Why did they want to know?" He raised his head off the pillow to face her?

"I don't *know*. But they asked if I knew that you had a wife and five children in Pennsylvania."

"Oh no," he groaned, and buried his face in the pillow.

"Well, *do you*? You told me you had *two* children.,"

He raised his head again, and she thought he looked even more ill as he answered, "Yes, Mary and I have five children, four girls and a boy. I … I don't know why I told you just two. They're all good kids and I miss them. As soon as I get a little stronger I want to go see them again." His voice got weaker, and he was quiet.

But soon he rallied and asked, "Who were these men? What did they look like?"

"The one who did the talking was quite heavy, could have been your age or a little older, and had dark hair. The other man was thin, and a little younger. *He* didn't say a word, but the one who spoke seemed very angry."

"I bet it was Mary's brother, but how did he find out where we live? Well, don't worry about it. I don't think they'll come back. But they *will* tell Mary."

Jenny heard him groan again as he turned over and was soon snoring heavily. *Yes, he could sleep!* Finally, from sheer exhaustion, she too, dozed off.

CHAPTER 3

Two weeks after the shocking phone call, Andy came running with the mail calling, "Look, a letter from Papa!"

Mama's hand shook as she read it to herself first, while the children begged, "What does he say? Read it out loud!"

"Dear Mary, I am out of the hospital now and feeling stronger every day. I'll be coming home on the bus next Tuesday." And that was all.

"Papa's coming home. Papa's coming home," we cried, hardly able to wait until Tuesday. Papa was coming home. That seemed so right. We didn't understand Mama's pale face and her silence as she stood there holding the letter.

• • • • •

When Papa came walking from the bus, immaculate in his blue pin-striped suit and solid blue tie, he walked slowly and not so straight and confident as usual. I saw him first. "Hi, Papa," I called, running out and taking his hand.

"Amanda, you look so pretty. How are you? Did you have a good day in school?"

"Sure. We got our report cards and I got all A's except for a C in history."

Once in the house Papa sat down. He looked tired. I remembered the phone call, but was hardly able to believe it was true. No one said anything to Papa about it, but Mama's silence spoke of discomfort. Papa and Mama never looked one another in the eye as Mama, dressed as usual in her caped dress and wearing her prayer covering, put the mashed potatoes and gravy, green beans and cornbread on the table. As we all sat down to eat, only Sarah and Nancy chatted away as usual, unaware of the tension. I loved mashed potatoes, but somehow I found it hard to swallow them tonight.

We had just finished eating supper when a car drove in the lane with Uncle Jesse and Uncle Bob in it. Mama told us children to go upstairs. Then she invited her brother, Jesse, and her sister's husband, Bob, to come in. We all huddled around the register above the kitchen stove, straining to hear the conversation below. We couldn't hear enough to know what transpired.

After a while we heard the car start up and we knew the coast was clear. We all rushed downstairs and found Papa missing.

"Where's Papa?" We chorused.

Mama hesitated and looked toward the door.

"Uncle Jesse insisted he go with him. They are taking him back to New Jersey."

We all cried, "But why? He is our Papa. He belongs here!"

And I demanded tearfully, "How did Uncle Jesse know Papa was here?"

"Well," Mama tried to explain, "I told my mother what they said at the hospital. She told my brother and he went over to New Jersey and found out that Papa is living there with another woman and has two children there."

"But he's *our* Papa. He belongs to *us*." I cried.

"They should make him stay *here,*" agreed Beth. "It's not fair!"

Mama tried to justify her brother's action. "Uncle Jesse doesn't think Papa should come here when he's living with another woman."

No words from Mama, however, could comfort us desolate children, and Mama cried with us, as, on pillows soaked with tears, we finally got quiet.

But sleep? I shared the bed with Beth, and after a long silence I whispered, "Are you sleeping?"

"No," she said. "I can't sleep for thinking about Papa and what happened."

"Me too," I said.

It was after midnight when we finally fell asleep.

We woke up the next morning and it seemed like a bad dream. I looked at Beth. "Can you believe what happened last night?" I asked.

"I wish we could let him know we want him back," she said.

"Let's write him a letter."

"Yes, let's," I said.

"Well, we have to get up and go to school. Let's try to be normal and just pray," said the practical and spiritually minded Beth.

So we got dressed and went downstairs. Mama looked sick. But somehow we ate breakfast and all got out in time to get on the school bus.

CHAPTER 4

Remembering the events of the night before, Mary awoke with a splitting headache. The children were so angry about Jesse's taking Steve away, and for her it made the separation from Steve seem so final!

She was used to getting along without him, but had hoped things would soon be different.

Mary managed to get up and see the children off to school, and five-year-old Nancy seemed content to play by herself. *Dear innocent Nancy! She doesn't realize the turmoil going on in the family. She doesn't even question why I need to go lie down.*

It was not the first time Mama got a migraine headache.

Now that she knew where Steve lived and had an address, she could write to him. She decided to write him and let him know how she and the children felt. Late that night after the children were in bed, with her head still throbbing, she wrote:

Dear Steve, The children and I cried and cried after Jesse took you away last night, and I woke up with a headache this morning. I don't know if Jesse explained to you why he did it, but he was adamant that you should not be here with me when you lived with another woman.

I know he was angry, and perhaps he did not talk to you. I wonder what you said and how you felt on that two hour trip to New Jersey last night. The whole situation really distresses the children and me.

I must confess, though, that even before you went to the hospital I was suspicious that you were having an affair, but of course couldn't prove it. Why did our marriage have to turn out like this?

Please write and tell us how you are and what you plan to do. Can you come back and make everything right?

Love, Mary

Mary felt better after she had written. Now she eagerly awaited a reply, which arrived two weeks later.

Dear Mary, Thanks for writing. Yes, Jesse was mad. He didn't talk to me the whole way to New Jersey. It was a horrible night.

Jenny welcomed me back, however, and she and her family are all so nice to me I cannot leave them now. Jenny was never married, and just came out of the Catholic convent before I met her. Our two girls are the cutest little things you ever saw.

I am sending you a check for $15.00. I should be able to send you more soon.

Keep in touch, Steve

Mary was glad for the letter and the money but at the same time furious. *The very idea of his saying they are "the cutest little things you ever saw."* This letter she did not share with the children. She told her mother, "Can you imagine his having the nerve to say that to me? What about my children? He always thought they were cute." Grandma Sauder tried to console Mary, but did not succeed in comforting her.

"Maybe I should take an aspirin," she said to herself, but then decided, "No, I'll just get to work." She jerked out the ironing board and put her energy into pressing the clothes. Then she strode out to the garden, chopped at the weeds, and planted another row of beans.

While she worked, she reflected on the past, and got to wondering why Steve turned out the way he did. Steve and she both grew up in Mennonite farm families with similar values. Yet something seemed to be lacking in the relationship between Steve and his father. She recalled some things Steve's sister had told her about how it went at home.

• • • • •

Steve grew up on a farm, the oldest of ten children. His mother thought Steve did no wrong, and the other children considered him Mama's pet.

One day when Steve came in from feeding the calves,

Pop, as he called his father, scolded him, "Steve, you spilled too much feed beside the trough. Don't you know that feed is expensive?"

Steve didn't answer, and Pop went on to something about what his brother had done that didn't please him.

Steve went to his mother after Pop left the kitchen. "Why does Pop always find something to fuss about? I didn't drop much of the precious grain."

Mom consoled her son, "Don't mind Pop. He criticizes lots of stuff I do, too. He is so concerned about money.

"What I wish for," said Steve "is a little encouragement from him. I guess you wish for that, too. Well, let's stick together, Mom. I know you like what I do."

Soon after Steve turned sixteen, Pop bought him a new car, a Willys Knight, no less. Top of the line! Pop bought the other boys cars, too, when they turned sixteen. Then he expected the boys to use the cars as he dictated, to do errands that helped bring in profit, not just for pleasure driving.

When Steve got a job away from home, however, he was out from under Pop's jurisdiction. One job took him fifty miles from home, necessitating his boarding away from home. Then he made friends with fellows who had different values from what he had been taught. Steve learned to know the world of movies, a bit of drinking, and smoking. When he came home he told one of his younger brothers about his adventures, but he didn't want to hurt his mother, so he kept his doings all secret from his parents.

He continued going to the Mennonite Church on weekends, and dated Mennonite girls to please his mother.

• • • • •

At the end of the bean row Mary noticed two sparrows sitting on the fence.

"You remember that God sees when a sparrow falls?" she asked herself. "Yes, and I know that my Lord will never leave or forsake me. He'll help me take care of the children."

This calming thought, together with working in the fresh air, tempered her emotions and her headache left. She found strength to go into the house and be her cheerful self as she prepared supper for the children.

The Sunday after that letter came, Mother's sister Annie and her husband came to visit the Johns family. They gave Mary $10.00, and brought homemade cheese and butter. Mary's family helped her out a lot during the next years, as Papa only sent about $15.00 a month.

One day when Grandma Sauder was visiting and helping Mary, they noticed that a house down the street was going to be sold on public auction. Grandma said to Mary, “Maybe I should buy that house so you don’t have to pay rent. What do you think it will bring at auction?”

“I have no idea,” said Mary. “Oh Mother, that would be wonderful if you could buy us a place. Let’s go look at it.”

So Mary and her mother went to see it. The house was large, well built, and in good condition, but did not have any electricity or running water. It had a pump outside over a well, and a small rain water pump inside.

The elderly couple had both died, and the house stood empty. Located by a stream, with apple trees, pear trees, grape vines on large arbors, its features attracted Mary. She thought of ways she might use the two-story shed, corn crib, chicken house and, of course, the large yard and garden. The outside toilet would need to suffice until they saved money for indoor plumbing.

“What do you think, Mary? Could you manage for a while without electricity?”

“Of course, we did without it for a while on the farm.”

“I’ll ask lawyer Witmer what he thinks it might bring at the sale. I’d like to buy it, but I wonder how that would affect Steve. Will he keep giving you as much money as he does if he knows you don’t need to pay rent?”

A week later, Grandma Sauder came with the answer from the Mennonite lawyer. "Mary, he thinks it might bring $5,000 or $6,000. I don't think I should pay that much, but he said he will come with me to the sale. I didn't ask him to do that, but I appreciate it."

When Mary told the children about this possibility, they jumped up and down for joy. The day of the public auction Mary went with her mother and the lawyer. The bidding stopped after Grandma's nod for $4000. Grandma Sauder promised Mary to count half that amount as a gift toward inheritance, and title it in her own name so that Steve cannot claim it.

Mary dreaded going through the process of moving again, but she looked forward to living in a house of her own. She hoped that somehow she could eventually buy the other half. That night she knelt beside her bed as usual and prayed, "God, you do care about us. Thank you for helping us through the kindness of my mother."

CHAPTER 5

Back on the farm, we children had known the security of Papa's presence. I liked our home with the large yard and garden, but sometimes when I felt sad about Papa being away, my thoughts went back to earlier days when Papa always came home in the evening. Beth, Andy, Sarah, and I talked together about those days, too. Some things we remembered, and other parts of the story we heard from Mama.

• • • • •

Papa and Mama had started out in 1926 on a 45-acre farm owned by Grandpa Johns. Beth, Andy, Sarah, and I were all born in the big farm house. We ate meals together around the long table with rounded leaves which could be folded down at each end. We had lots of space to play in the huge kitchen with flowered wall paper, green linoleum on the floor, and a wood and coal burning cook stove. One time Beth and Andy played "farm" by turning the table up on end to make a barn. But "Oops!" the leaf broke off!

Sometimes I went along with Andy and Papa to the big barn and watched while Papa milked the cows. "Open your mouth," Papa said to Andy. Then he squirted milk right into his mouth.

Wanting to be like my older brother, I said, "Me too, Papa." So Papa squirted milk at me, but I moved a little and it went down on my chin.

I liked the big porch with the two-seated wooden swing held by chains fastened in the roof. I often watched as my cousin, Marie, scrubbed the porch clean. Mama was particular, and Marie worked hard as Mama's helper. But that big porch and banister turned out to be a hazard, too.

Mama often told the story about Andy's fall:

> One day when Marie was watching the children, the adventuresome Andy, fifteen months old, climbed up on the banister of the big porch. He called, "Papa," as Papa came up the walk toward the house.
>
> "Andy, be careful!" Papa ran, but got there too late to catch the little boy who landed on the cement pavement. He lay there limp, blood collecting under his head. Papa picked him up and cried, "Mary, come quick! Andy's hurt real bad." Mama held Andy while Papa drove them to the hospital seven miles away. Five-year-old Beth cried and Marie tried to comfort her while holding me. I was only

two-months old.

"It's good Papa was here when Andy fell," said the tearful Beth. "Mama and Papa will soon come back, won't they?" She sniffed and wiped her tears.

In the hospital, the doctor said, "Fractured skull. He'll need to stay for a few days." Mama tearfully left Andy with the nurses and joined Papa to come back home to us. To everyone's relief, Andy soon recovered and romped around with as much curiosity and daring as before.

• • • • •

Beth started first grade at the one-room school about a mile away from the farm. Two years later, Andy started. When Beth was in third grade and Andy in first, Beth got sick one day and the teacher took her home. When Andy found out about this, he got up out of his seat, headed for the door and ran all the way home. He wasn't staying in school without his big sister!

"But what about your lunch box and coat?" asked Mother.

"I'll get them for Andy," I volunteered. So with some hesitancy, Mama allowed me, the brave five-year-old, to walk to the school to get Andy's coat and lunch box.

The Great Depression of the late 1920s and early 1930s made it difficult for Papa to make ends meet financially.

"The potato crop is doing well, Mary. But I can only get fifty cents a bushel. I can't make a living on that. What do you think if we started raising chickens?"

"Well, that might be okay. But where will you sell them?"

"I know the market in Philadelphia would buy them," Steve replied.

"Oh, but then you'd be away a lot, and we'd need to tend the cows and chickens while you're gone. I don't like that idea. But if that's the only way, I guess we'll do the best we can."

Papa did sell chickens in Philadelphia for awhile, but soon that seemed like more work than it was worth. So he got a part-time job at a store downtown. His boss found him to be a good salesman, and promoted him to selling vacuum cleaners to people in their homes. He loved getting out and meeting people. His charisma as a "people person" led him to success in a way he'd never known working for his father on the farm. Salesmanship was a "natural" for Papa. Thus began Papa's rest of his life career as a traveling salesman.

Papa's new career also led us away from the farm. Soon after I turned six, our family moved from the farm to a small rented house in the suburbs of the city. I didn't mind this, but Sarah, only three, stood there by the door while we started to unpack our things. She refused to take off her little blue coat and cap. "I want to go home!" she cried. Then Beth took her by the hand and explained to her that this was home. When she saw Mama in the kitchen preparing dinner, she finally took off her coat and started wandering about the house.

For Andy and me, moving to the "new" house was a great adventure. We explored it from attic to cellar. We found one bedroom for Beth, Sarah, and me, and the one across the hall suited Andy just fine. Then we went outside to investigate.

"Not much space to play," Andy observed. A fence divided the small back yard from that of the landlord who lived in the other half of the house. A large cherry tree stood near the fence.

"Look, there are cherry blossoms on this tree. Maybe we'll have cherries to eat," observed Beth.

"How do you know it's a cherry tree? I asked.

"Well, the blossoms and the bark look just like the big cherry tree we had on the farm." The cherries ripened and Mama canned 27 quarts.

When September came, Beth, Andy, and I, walked a quarter mile on a path from our street over to the consolidated school, where I started first grade. On May Day, I took part in wrapping the colored streamers around the Maypole. I liked my teacher and got along well in school. One day the teacher assigned us different seats. A nice little boy then sat in front of me. After we all got settled in our new locations, the boy turned around and smiled at me. The teacher came and whispered in my ear, "When he does that, you just tell him to turn around." I didn't want to do that, because I liked the boy and was glad to have him smile at me.

When the big carnival came to a nearby lot, Papa gave each of us a whole nickel to spend. I got an ice cream cone with my nickel. Andy got cotton candy. We rode the merry-go-round, rode a pony, played some games, and watched the animals. Then we hurried home to tell Papa and Mama all about it.

After selling vacuum cleaners, Papa got a job as an automobile salesman. This job allowed him to drive a demonstration car and use it for the family. "Look at the shiny green car I brought home today," he announced.

Soon Andy and I were crawling all over the car. "Let's go for a ride in it. Can we, Papa?" Andy asked.

"Okay, we can go for a short ride before supper," Papa said.

"Look, it has a rumble seat. Can we ride in that?

"Hop in," was all Papa needed to say.

Mama wasn't sure if I should go because I had just recovered from the measles, but she smiled and waved as she watched us leave.

I should have heeded Mama's caution. The joy ride had a down side for me. I developed a severe earache from riding in the open air. Nothing seemed to relieve my pain, so finally Papa took me to the doctor.

"She'll need to go to the hospital for a mastoid operation," I heard the doctor tell Papa.

"What is a mastoid operation?" I cried.

The doctor explained to me that he needed to take the infection out so my ear would not hurt any more. So I had no choice, but to be put to bed in the hospital. They gave me something to make me sleep while the doctor operated.

Papa and Mama both stood beside my bed when I woke up. I complained, "I can't get this cap off." The "cap" was a large bandage around my head. I cried a lot and didn't want Mama to leave. Once when Papa brought Mama in, I told her, "I was crying for you and the nurse said, 'If you don't stop crying, I'll tell your mother not to come in,' so I stopped."

That hospital stay with all the attention I got helped me get over my bashfulness. The doctor humored me along, "I like to see your dimples when you smile," he said. Then I smiled all the more.

The next summer Papa found a house to rent in the city. I asked, "Why are we going to move again, Mama? I like it here."

Mama hesitated. "Well, Papa didn't pay the rent for the last couple of months and the landlord says we must move."

"Then we'll have to go to a new school and leave our playmates." I said. Beth, Andy, and I, cried at the thought, but our sadness didn't change the fact.

So we moved to center city. The house looked just like all the other houses joined together in a row with a small narrow alley along the side to get from the sidewalk to the back yard. The house was tall and narrow with a basement, a first floor with living room inside the front door, then a small dining room and a fairly good sized kitchen. Again Andy and I explored the "new" house. We ran up the steps to see what the bedrooms looked like. There was a bathroom upstairs and three small bedrooms.

"Let's leave the attic until later," said Andy. "I want to see what the outside is like."

"Not much space to play. Just like the other place. And not even a cherry tree!" But what kind of tree is this? Look, it has small apples on it. Let's try one."

"Ooh, it's sour. I wonder if Mama knows what it is."

We took a few of the apples in to Mama, who was busy putting things into the cupboards in the kitchen. "They look like crab apples," she said.

Then we unpacked our own clothes, books, and the few toys we had brought along, and soon we felt at home in the "new" house.

During my second year in the school just two city blocks away, I became ill with scarlet fever. The board of health put a big pink sign on the front door which announced that we were quarantined. Now Andy and Beth had to stay home from school, too, even though they were not sick. I had to stay in one room upstairs. When Papa came home from work, he peered in at me from the door.

"Papa, come on in. I want to talk with you," I invited.

"Amanda, I'm sorry, but the rules are that if I come into your room when you are sick I may not go to work."

Then instead of Papa coming in and sitting on my bed, he just talked with me from the door. I didn't like that, but I knew he needed to go to work, so I didn't cry about it.

I had barely gotten over the scarlet fever before Andy and Beth got mumps. Then we had the quarantine sign on the door again, I had to stay home from school when I was not sick. When the placard finally came off the front door we all returned to school.

However, after only a half day in school, I felt my neck where it hurt and it was beginning to swell up. I shyly went to my teacher and told her. She looked at me and immediately said, "Mumps." So I had to go home and miss school for another two weeks.

I cried a lot, not so much for the pain, but because I loved school, and didn't want to stay home. In spite of missing a lot of school, I learned to read well. The teacher sometimes told the children, "If you come to a word you don't know, you may go and ask Amanda." This saved the teacher some interruptions while she taught the other reading groups. I told Papa all about it, and he said he was proud of me. It was always rewarding to tell Papa if I did well in school.

After school Mama usually had work for us to do.

"I need some help here," she'd say. She set the big dishpan of potatoes in the sink. "Beth and Amanda, you can peel these potatoes while I get the rest of the meal ready. Andy you can set the table. Papa will soon be home."

Beth got out the knives and I helped wash the potatoes. We learned to make work into fun. Peeling potatoes, a sometimes boring job, brought out our creativity. When Beth peeled the first potato, it looked perfect. But when she cut it in half we saw it had brown spots inside.

"This potato is like a hypocrite," she said. "It looks good on the outside but is sinful inside." Then I found one that had wrinkles on the skin. But after I peeled it and cut it I found it to be perfect inside.

"See?" Beth said, "This one is like people who aren't attractive, but are really good at heart." Beth had a way of turning our thoughts into worthwhile channels.

"Let's sing our 'potato song,'" said Amanda. "I'm so happy, so very happy.'"

Beth led out in one song after another from memory. "I

have the joy, joy, joy, joy, down in my heart." Then, "Every day with Jesus is sweeter than the day before," and on and on until soon the potatoes were all peeled and in the pot cooking.

We had songs for other occasions, too, such as, "Peace, Be Still," during thunderstorms.

Papa continued selling Pontiacs, and seemed to be doing well, but never seemed to have much money for Mama. I found Mama crying one evening. Mama seldom allowed us to see her crying or to hear her complaining about things. But this time her load must've overwhelmed her. It alarmed me to find her in tears. I asked, "Mama, what's the matter?"

"Oh Amanda, I'll be all right, but I just don't see how we'll have enough money for the new baby."

"A new baby? Hey Andy," I called. "We're going to have a new baby." We all thought that would be fun.

One day when we were out for a drive, Papa asked, "If we have a little boy, what are we going to call him?"

"How about Ronnie?" suggested Andy.

"No, not Ronnie. Maybe John," I piped up"

However, on June 16 right after school ended, instead of a boy, Mama gave birth to a healthy baby girl. We children liked the name Nancy after my best friend up the street. Mama liked that, too, so Nancy it was. To please Papa, Nancy was given the middle name, Ella, after Grandma Johns.

We all competed for turns to hold Baby Nancy. Mama, too, appeared to be happy since the baby was born and she lavished her love on Nancy. A few days later Papa asked Andy, "How would you like to spend some time this summer helping Grandpa and Uncle Leroy on the farm?"

"You mean I'd stay there overnight and eat there with Grandma and Grandpa? I think I'd like that. Maybe I'll be a farmer!"

"Can I go too?" I piped up.

Papa looked at Mama. "Well, I have Beth here to help me with Sarah and Nancy, so I guess Amanda can go, too, that is if Grandma wants her."

After a teary goodbye, Andy and I joyfully rode with Papa in the sleek blue Pontiac he drove as his demonstration car. We didn't like leaving Mama and Baby Nancy, but the excitement of being on the farm took over. I didn't know this at the time, but our being away helped out financially, as Mama had two less mouths to feed.

Papa was the oldest in a family of ten. His younger siblings, Henry, Leroy, Ellen, and Molly, who still lived at home, all helped make life on the farm interesting for Andy and me. One day Aunt Ellen challenged me, "Amanda, here is a poem I like. Maybe you could memorize it." I looked at this long poem.

"I don't know if I can, but I will try."

"If you can memorize this whole poem, I'll give you a penny for each verse."

That did it. I got busy and learned all 23 eight line verses of "Tommy's Prayer." Then Aunt Ellen gave me twenty three cents, a fabulous amount!

"Thank you," I said. "I never had that much money all of my own."

Andy liked working on the dairy farm, and we both enjoyed playing in the orchard. The summer turned out to be a good experience for us. Papa came to pick us up and we quickly said goodbye to everyone on the farm and chattered the whole way home.

"We liked the farm, Papa. And Grandma made the best pies," I said.

"Andy, what did you like best?" Papa asked.

"I really liked the cows. Uncle Leroy taught me how to milk. He said they are getting milking machines soon, and then they won't have to milk like we did. You have to squeeze the teats just right. I liked squirting the milk into the bucket, and sometimes putting some in little pans for the cats."

"I liked playing games with Aunt Molly, too, didn't you, Andy?

"We liked almost everything, but sometimes we felt a little homesick," Andy admitted.

"I know. And I can hardly wait to see Baby Nancy and Mama," I said.

When we got home to our little house in the city, we ran up the steps and shouted, "Hey, we're home! Where's Mama? Oh, Baby Nancy grew. Look at her, Andy."

We both reached for her, but I got her first. "Ah, isn't she the cutest baby you ever saw!"

Soon it was time to go back to school. But wait! "Oh, no! Don't tell me we have to go to a new school again," I complained.

"Yes," Beth explained. She had learned all about it before we got home. "Papa got behind with the rent again, so we have to move. Mama doesn't like it, but she has no choice. Neither do we. Papa found a little house out in the country."

Papa borrowed a truck and helped to load the furniture. Mama had everything neatly packed before the truck arrived. Papa took all of us in the car while someone else drove the truck. And so it was that we moved again, started a new school again, and once again explored a "new" house. This one used to be a schoolhouse. A whole lot of cement steps led up to the small front porch. This was smaller than any house we lived in yet. We had more play space outside, though, and what looked like it could be a garden. But since we moved so near the end of the summer, Mama saw no point in planting anything. Besides, the soil was stony and claylike.

We rode a bus to school—a new experience for us as we had walked to school at the other places.

"Hurry, it's time for the school bus," came the usual cry. We all scurried up the hill to the bus stop. One day when I got to school and took off my coat, I found I was wearing my apron. How embarrassing! I quickly took it off and stuffed it into my coat pocket.

This school was part of the college campus, and we had student teachers, as well as a homeroom teacher.

Andy and I got the job of carrying milk from the farm down at the bottom of the hill. I liked that because along the way we could see my best friend, who lived on the farm. Our house stood along a rather long hill, which provided an excellent track in winter for sledding. Even Mama liked to come out and take a sled ride down the long hill.

But again our family had to leave our friends and move, this time before the school year ended. That's when we moved to the place with a large garden along the busy highway.

CHAPTER 6

For a long time after the night when Uncle Jesse took Papa back to New Jersey, my siblings and I didn't see Papa. Every night we all knelt by our beds and earnestly beseeched our Heavenly Father, "Please help Papa to become a Christian. And please help him to come home to stay." That simple prayer was most sincere. In our innocence and faith, we thought if Papa just became a Christian, that would solve all of our problems and we'd be a big happy family.

Then two months before our family moved to the house Grandma bought, Papa started to come see us again. On that first visit, not understanding the awkwardness this created for Mama, we children ran out to greet him with cheers and hugs. Mama treated him as a guest, setting out a simple but nourishing meal consisting of chicken, potatoes, green beans, and coleslaw. The vegetables, of course, came from our own garden. Papa, a good pretender, acted like nothing had changed. We children found it hard to believe that Papa lived with another family.

On the second visit Papa came with a surprise. Andy was upstairs working on a model airplane. Papa called, "Andy, look what I brought you."

Andy hopped down the stairs two at a time. "It's out here in the driveway." Papa said as he led the way.

"Wow! A bike! For me?"

"Yes, it's for you Andy. Now listen, son. Don't ride after dark. And always let your mother know where you are going and when you will be home."

Two rules from Papa, and that was it. "I can hardly believe it is true," said Andy. "My own black and white, full-sized bike!" He quickly mounted and rode up and down the driveway. I soon learned to ride the bike, too, and competed for turns.

Now with a bicycle, Andy took on a paper route. I also helped to fold the papers and deliver them. We liked that job. Andy kept a small percentage of his profit, but Mother needed most of the money for food and clothing for the family, and Andy willingly turned it over.

In mid summer, we moved to the "new" house by the stream. I followed Andy up the narrow stairway to the attic to explore. "Look, Amanda, here's an old coal oil lamp. And what's this?"

"It looks like a bed, but what an odd one. See these little knobs along the bed rails? And here are some ropes. It looks like the ropes fit around these little pegs. Is there such a thing as a rope bed?" I asked.

"And here's a big thick bag stuffed with feathers. That must be the mattress. Let's see what else the old people left here. Look at all these jars and crocks. They're probably antiques. Amanda, do you think we could get money for them?"

"Maybe we can. But look, here's a big wooden box with a tight lid." With some difficulty we pried the top off. "Look Andy, here's an old doll, a marble roller, and some old picture post cards, and even some books. We'll have to show these to Beth."

An old stool, several chairs, and an old table inspired the idea for a secret attic hideout. "But it's hot up here. Let's go see what treasures we can find in the cellar," said Andy.

First we peeked in each of the four bedrooms, which all opened into the large central hall. Then we ran down the big open stairway to the hallway on the first floor. To the left of the big front door was a good-sized living room, and to the right a dining room with a pot belly stove for heat. At the end of the hall was the entrance to the large kitchen with a wood and coal burning cook stove. To the right was another small room with a coal oil stove for cooking, and a hand-operated rain water pump and a trough. One of Mama's sisters gave us a bathtub, which we walled in to make a "bathroom" in half of that little room. A water hookup to the tub did not exist, so we drained the water from the tub into a low pan and dumped it into the trough by the rain water pump. Later we got running water in the bathroom and even had a flush toilet and a washbowl in that little room. Meanwhile, we used the "outhouse" toilet. Instead of going out at night we used a chamber bucket upstairs.

From the kitchen a door led to the basement. Down the narrow dark stairway we hurried.

"Eeee-eeek," I shrieked, "there went a big rat across the floor. Oooo I hate rats. Let's get out of here."

I ran back up the steps, and it was a long time before Andy convinced me to come down and explore further in the cellar.

But he *did* get me to go out and see what the barn had to offer. I made sure to bang on the door to scare away any rodents that might be hiding in this place long uninhabited by humans. The entry way with cement floor led to the dirt floor garage. A wooden stairway led to a loft above. I especially liked that part with the slanted roof, many rafters which could serve as shelves, and lots of old boxes for furniture.

"Wow, this will make a better fun hideout than the attic," I decided.

Andy agreed, as we explored the other barn. "And over here we could keep some chickens, or maybe even a goat," he said.

Next we explored the grounds. Along the west side of the property ran a small stream. "Look at this," I called to Andy. "I think this is watercress. That's good to eat. I remember when Grandma Sauder gave us some, and we sprinkled salt on it and put it in between two slices of butter bread for a sandwich. Yum!"

• • • • •

Further up the stream, we found a large bush with small green berries. "These look like elderberries. Mama can make good pies and jam from them."

Andy was studying the stream. "I think it is deep enough here that we can float a boat."

And later on Andy did make a boat with the help of cousins who lived on the other side of the stream. They used an old door for the bottom. When heavy rains came, the yard got flooded and they put the boat in the "pond" in the yard. What fun! They also used it in the stream when the water was high enough.

The "new" place had an even larger garden and yard than the rented house. So another way we helped earn money was to sell vegetables. Mother knew how to raise wonderful potatoes, tomatoes, sweet corn, cabbage, lima beans, and celery. Mother expected us children to help in the garden—pulling weeds and hoeing corn, but Mother did most of the harvesting herself.

When weeds got ahead of us and the ground was hard, we enjoyed an adventure. "Andy and Amanda," Mama called. We stopped our play and listened. "Do you think you could go back to the farm and borrow a horse and harrow from the Amish people?

"We can try." So we walked back the quarter-mile lane to our friendly Amish neighbors and told them what Mother wanted to do.

"Do you think you can handle the horse?" they questioned.

"We'll try. You can tell us how." So with directions about what to say and how to pull the reins, we led the old mule out the lane to our place. I led the mule holding the rein close to the head while Andy held the harrow up by the handles so it rode on the one wheel. In the garden, Andy rode the mule while Mother held the harrow as it cultivated between the rows of corn and beans.

When the sweet corn became plentiful, Andy rigged up a big sign to place out along the busy highway. "Look at this," he said. "Amanda, can you paint a picture of an ear of corn on here?"

• • • • •

Corn was the main attraction for passers by. So we wrote "Sweet Corn" in big letters, and then I painted a picture of an ear of corn on it. As soon as we got the sign out, people started to stop. "How much is the corn?"

"Fifty cents a dozen," we announced. We charged more or less depending on the quality and quantity available. "We also have tomatoes, cabbage, and cucumbers today," I said. I liked selling to people who stopped to buy, rather than going from door to door, which we also did sometimes.

In addition to the paper route and selling garden things, Andy and I went into business selling candy bars from door to door.

"I don't like asking people to buy things," I said, "but I know we need the money." I'm not sure how much profit we made, for we ate a Milky Way bar now and then.

Papa continued to come home every month or so for a short visit. When he came he often handed Mama $15.00 cash. In between he sometimes sent a check in the mail for $10.00 or $15.00. Relatives helped us during these difficult times. The storekeeper gave special bargains; the baker brought day- old bread. Somehow Mama kept food on the table. We children never went hungry even though money was never plentiful.

When Christmas time came that year, we all wondered what Papa would do. He usually came and took Mother and all of us children to Grandpa and Grandma Johns's for the big family Christmas dinner. The word had gotten around to Papa's family that Papa lived with another woman. Among Mennonites, divorce and separations were rare, and something you didn't talk much about. It was not only a great embarrassment for Mama and us, but also for Papa's parents and siblings.

To Mama's surprise, but to our delight, Papa came and took us to the Christmas dinner. Grandma and Grandpa Johns treated him as part of the family, but with reserve. Grandma looked sober when she greeted him. But Papa behaved as usual, telling stories about his work, and asking others about theirs. He asked Uncle Leroy, Papa's youngest brother who still lived at home on the farm, "How many cows are you milking now? How do you like the new barn? Is it better than the old one that burned down?"

He even told Aunt Ellen, "That's a pretty dress you are wearing." She looked a little embarrassed, but pleased. Dressing nice was important to all of Papa's family.

Tantalizing smells from Grandma's dinner drew us all to the dining room and the long table, set with Grandma's best china and silverware. We could hardly wait, but it took some time until everyone found their place—adults around the big table in the dining room, and we children in the kitchen with our cousins and Aunt Molly, Papa's youngest sister. Before we could eat, we all bowed our heads for silent prayer and waited until we heard movement in the other room. Amidst the chatter, we passed first of all bread, butter and jam, then the turkey, filling, mashed potatoes, gravy, lima beans and corn, cranberry sauce and homegrown celery.

"Don't forget to save room for the dessert," Aunt Molly warned. But I always found room in my tummy for Grandma's chocolate cake with caramel icing!

Finally satisfied, and maybe even stuffed, we left the table. "What do you want to play?" Aunt Molly asked. Aunt Molly seemed more like a cousin, being only three years older than Beth.

"Parcheesi," Beth suggested.

"How about dominoes?" I suggested.

"I'd like to play checkers," said Andy. So we all got busy playing various games. But we gladly stopped our games and gathered in the living room when Grandpa decided to hand out the Christmas gifts. He went around and gave each of his grandchildren a quarter, and all his children a dollar bill. We all treasured that bit of wealth!

• • • • •

Beth faced a difficult decision after her junior year in high school. "How can I spend money which we don't have in order to go to the Mennonite school? And I surely don't want to go to the public school." The Mennonite school had opened the year Beth started as a freshman. We say that Beth prayed the Christian school into being. She attended for three years. Where the money came from, I don't know. But after her third year, she quit to earn money for the family. Beth was a good student, and graduating from high school seemed like the right thing for her to do. But she willingly quit school and got a job at a dry cleaning plant.

For a young conscientious Mennonite seventeen-year-old girl, working at the plant brought many challenges to Beth One coworker smoked, another was divorced from her husband, and some used dirty language. All this shocked Beth. She came home from work exhausted, not only from the physical labor, but tired emotionally. She prayed regularly for her coworkers and somehow survived working there for several years until she found a better job working in the kitchen of the Christian high school. There she made many friends, and enjoyed her work.

When it came time for me to go to high school, I knew Mama could not afford to send me to the Mennonite School.

"Mama," I proposed one day, "I think I could go to the public high school, at least for the first two years. What do you think?"

Mama hesitated a bit, and then answered, "That might be a good idea. I wish you could go to the Mennonite school, but … I believe you will do alright in public school."

However, just before school began, the minister from our church came and asked me, "Amanda, how would you like to go to the Mennonite high school?"

"I'd love to," I answered. "But we don't have the money, so I'm going to the public school."

"But what if someone paid your way?"

Then I perked up. The pastor continued, "Someone has offered to pay your way to attend the Mennonite high school. They see you as a young person with possibilities. They are not relatives, and they wish to remain anonymous."

"That would be wonderful! I really wanted to go to the Mennonite school. Yes, I'll accept that offer. You can't tell me who it is? Well, tell them a most grateful thank you from me. I'll try to do well in school."

It didn't take long for me to change my plans. I gladly registered as a freshman in the Mennonite high school. And I never did learn the identity of the kind person or persons who paid my way. I'm sure they must have watched me, and I hope I didn't disappoint them.

In school I did not want my classmates to know that my father and mother were separated, and found it difficult to explain the situation to my friends.

When Papa was with Mama and us children, he always kept his two families separate, never calling me Julie, or Mama, Jenny. He did not talk about his second family when he was with us. Yet knowing about his double life created a certain amount of tension when he visited us. We didn't trust him anymore.

As I got older, I found it more difficult to share my personal life with Papa. He would ask about school, but it didn't seem like he really cared or understood how I felt. How could I tell him about how I enjoyed being in the home of my friend whose father led in family devotions every day, and how I wished I had a father like that?

My two high school friends, Laura, Ruth, and I, took turns going to each other's homes overnight. I loved being in Laura's home. Laura with her two brothers and five sisters together with their parents and Ruth and I, all sat around the large kitchen table to eat supper together. After supper Laura's father led the family in Bible reading, singing, and prayer. I could hardly sing for tears; it was so special to be singing with them. The whole family knelt down to pray. Ruth and I knelt with them. What a happy family! I confided in my friend Laura, "I wish my Papa came home every night and led family devotions like your father does."

Her response, "Well it just seems normal to me. I guess I didn't realize that other families don't do the same. What you say makes me more thankful for my father."

Papa didn't come to the school for my high school graduation, but he did remember me with a fine gift! On his next visit after my graduation he handed me a small box. "Oh, what's this?" I asked.

"That's something special for your graduation. Congratulations!"

I quickly opened the box and here was a beautiful watch in a gold case with little stones for the numbers—some clear and some red. "Wow! What a pretty watch! I never saw one like this. Thank you, thank you, Papa." I wanted to give him a hug, but I refrained, as that was something we just didn't do. Papa seemed pleased with my obvious pleasure and big smile.

• • • • •

In spite of everything, I still loved my Papa and was always glad to see him, but I wished he were my full time father.

CHAPTER 7

"Bong! Bong! Bong! Bong!"

"Oh, no," I sighed. "That must be Andy calling."

"Family devotions, everybody," yelled Andy.

Sometimes it seemed that Andy felt responsible to take over some "head of the house" duties in Papa's absence.

At the front door one rang the bell from the outside by pulling a knob which pulled a cable with a gong attached inside. The gong hitting the bell made a loud ringing sound. You could also pull on this cable from the inside and get the same effect. Andy got the "wise" idea to use this bell to call the family together *early* in the morning for family worship.

Not being a morning person, I shuffled down the stairs in housecoat and slippers with my eyes half open. "I know we should have devotions, but I wish you wouldn't call us so early," I complained.

Conscientious Beth tried to cooperate, as she and Andy both learned about "family devotions" at the Mennonite high school. Many times Andy did not get ready participation from the rest of us. A teenage brother leading family devotions just did not wield the authority of a father. Mama let it happen, but did not enforce it. Neither Mama nor Papa grew up in homes where their parents led daily family devotions, even though their families faithfully attended church and read the Bible.

Our mother never owned a car, nor did she have a driver's license. So when Papa was not home, our family depended on walking, riding the bus, or getting rides from other people. Somehow, we always managed to get to church and Sunday School. But when Summer Bible School started at the home church, we couldn't figure out a way to get there. No direct bus line, too far to walk. Then the Sunday before Bible School started, Mr. Ball came to Andy after church. "Would you and your sisters like to go to Bible School? I'd like to drive and take you."

"Oh, thanks," said Andy. "Beth and Amanda cried last night because we didn't have a way to go. What time shall we be at your house?"

Bright and early Monday morning and dressed in Sunday best, we all walked the fourth-mile to Mr. Ball's place. We all loved Bible School, all ten days of it. The singing was terrific, with "Uncle" James leading. We learned lots of new songs to add to our own repertoire. We memorized Scripture, too, and our Bible knowledge grew significantly. We kept going to Bible School every year. Our first year, it started in the forenoon, but later it changed to an evening school. I think it was easier to find teachers free to help in the evening. Later when Andy had a car, he could take us, and eventually, when I drove, I took other neighbor children along. I also taught Bible School many summers.

In addition to church and Bible School, Beth did a lot of reading and taught us younger children a lot about the Bible, and about right and wrong. One day Sarah, then in the 5th grade, came home with a ring. "My boyfriend gave it to me," she told Beth.

"Oh Sarah, you may not wear that. Don't you know it is a sin to wear jewelry?" Then she took the ring from Sarah and stepped on it smashing it. Later Sarah found it in the bedroom closet. In tears, Sarah cried to Beth, "What will I tell Mike when he sees I am not wearing the ring?"

Beth put her arms around the crying Sarah. "I'm sorry, Sarah," she said. "I guess you'll have to tell Mike your sister ruined the ring. You might as well tell him why I did it, too."

Mama's example of Christian faith spoke loudly, too. Often when I came home from school, as soon as I walked in the front door, I heard Mama's clear soprano voice singing a familiar hymn, like, "What a Friend We Have in Jesus." Singing became a special part of family life.

Mama often talked about how her mother used to play the organ and sing. "The hymns we sang taught us a lot of what we learned about spiritual things," she said. And for her children the same was true. The words of the hymns taught us good theology.

Mama prayed, too. We often saw her kneeling beside her bed at night, and somehow we knew she prayed for each of us.

At the Mennonite high school, we learned about modesty, social standards, and Christian behavior in general. The school held to stricter standards than the church. Girls' cape dresses had to be below the knees. Once I had a pretty dark green dress, a hand-me-down, which I wanted to wear for school, but it was too short. So Mama put a light green bias tape binding around the bottom to lengthen it. This did not embarrass me, as other girls wore strange looking borders around their dresses to lengthen them, too.

Boys were not allowed to wear neckties.

The matron taught strict "hands off" courtship standards to the girls. In separate meetings the hall manager taught the boys. Good Bible teaching at the school grounded us in the Christian faith, and served us well for years to come.

When Beth started working at a local dry cleaning plant, a whole new kind of worldly life shocked and troubled her. One day she came home crying. "It is awful at work. The women smoke, the boss uses curse words, and the lady who works beside me is divorced." This caused her much anxiety. But with all the turmoil, she remained steadfast in her faith and diligently prayed for the salvation of her coworkers.

• • • • •

Social life for the Johns family centered mostly on church activities. After Andy turned age sixteen, he learned to drive and soon he came home driving his own '41 Chevrolet.

We sisters all cheered. "Now you can take us to youth group activities."

So the sleek dark blue Chevy became the family car for church, Saturday and Sunday night youth gatherings, and a few treasured family outings. One summer Mama and all five of us children went to a music week at a Mennonite camp in western Pennsylvania. There we enjoyed learning to know other young people and families.

After high school, the Chevy took Andy on some dating, but he felt rejected by some of the girls he admired.

It was tough for a boy whose father and mother did not live together. Beth didn't seem to bother much about boyfriends.

I turned nineteen before I started dating. Ronnie, whom I liked in high school, never paid much attention to me. Toward the end of high school I began to like Matt. To my delight, a year after graduation, he came and asked me for a date. We dated for a while, and I really liked Matt. I even talked with him about my father, and that didn't seem to be a problem for him. But to my displeasure, the courtship only lasted six months.

After high school graduation, I thought about becoming a teacher. College was out of the question at that time due to lack of money. I got a good job in an insurance office, where I enjoyed my work and made life-long friends. My boss's generous praise and the regular pay raises helped me gain confidence.

The draft caught up with Andy, and he registered as a conscientious objector. To travel back and forth from his place of IW service in Connecticut, he bought a small Crosley. We sisters cried as we saw him off. "Do you think you will be safe in that little car?" I asked.

"Oh sure," said Andy. He smiled and waved as he drove off.

We missed our brother, and wrote to him regularly, and eagerly awaited his letters and return in frequent visits. We girls and Mother even went to Connecticut to visit him one time.

I bought the '41 Chevy from Andy. Then I could drive to and from my office job instead of riding the bus.

My younger sister, Nancy, got an idea she wanted a goat. So Mama left her get one. She kept it in the barn. For a while she fed it and took care of it, but when it came to milking the goat, the job fell to Mama. Mama didn't really like milking the goat, and taking care of the baby goat, and finally Nancy didn't care so much about it and the goats were sold.

One evening when I came home from work, I found Mother all worried. "Nancy did not get off the school bus. I thought maybe the teacher made her stay after school, but I called the school, and nobody knew anything about Nancy's whereabouts. Will you drive to the school and look for her?"

Just as it was getting dark I started out the driveway. But before I pulled out onto the highway, I saw Nancy walking up the steps. I parked the car and hurried back into the house. Nancy dropped her books on the table, and headed to the kitchen.

"I'm hungry. What's to eat around here?"

Then she noticed Mother, Sarah, and me all staring at her.

"What's wrong?" asked the carefree Nancy.

"What's wrong? Yes, what is wrong? Why didn't you come home on the school bus?" Mother questioned.

"Oh, Jody and I just decided it would be fun to walk home. We knew the way. I got here, didn't I?"

Everyone was so relieved to see her that Nancy escaped punishment. But when she came home the next day—on the bus—she sang a different tune.

"My teacher really gave it to us for walking home yesterday! Jody and I have to write a 200-word essay on the dangers of two eighth grade girls walking home from school."

And Nancy never again tried to walk home from school.

• • • • •

At age 23, after working in the office five years, I decided to go to college. I studied at the local state teachers college my first two years, which cost less than going to our church college, and allowed me to live at home. Then in my junior year, I transferred to our Mennonite college in another state, where I lived in the dorm and where I got my degree in elementary education. College turned out to be a good experience for me, as well as a growing experience. I grew socially and spiritually, and made many friends.

One weekend during the spring of my senior year in college, I came home for job interviews. The interview with the principal for the second grade opening in the public school went well. "Wouldn't it be neat to teach here only four miles from my home?" I thought. Then I had another interview with the principal of a Christian Day School for junior high age. I didn't know how I would like teaching that age group, but I thought I should not decide on the basis of the salary offered me. Before leaving for college I told my mother, "I'll probably take the junior high offer in the Christian Day School. I don't want money to be the deciding factor."

Back in my room at college I prayed and tried to discern what God wanted me to do. I opened my Bible and my eyes fell on a verse that said, "They that are whole need not a physician, but they that are sick."(Matt. 9:12b). Somehow this spoke clearly to me that the Lord wanted me in the public school. With a great sense of peace I signed and returned the contract for the second grade position in the public school near my home.

For my graduation, Papa brought Mama to the college along with Beth and Nancy. I was happy to have Papa there for this important event. I was proud to introduce my parents to my friends. They didn't all need to know that my parents didn't live together.

After Andy finished his time in Connecticut, he worked in New York City for a while. There he helped with the mission work and there he met Esther from Ohio, who also helped in the mission and worked at an office in the city. When Andy brought Esther to visit us, we all loved her right away. And then the exciting thing happened. They "left the cat out of the bag." Yes, they had a cat in a burlap bag, and left it out with the note tied to it, "Engaged: Andy and Esther."

When it came time for their wedding in Ohio, Andy invited Papa to the wedding. This began a series of trips when Papa drove the family to Ohio. In Ohio where people didn't know Papa, he attended the Mennonite church of Esther's family. Mama went along, too, although being with him did cause some embarrassment. When someone asked Papa, "Where do you live?" Without batting an eye, he answered, "We live in a small town near Lancaster, Pennsylvania." This seemed like a lie because he only visited us there. But we never had the nerve to confront him about it.

Two months after Andy's wedding, Sarah and John got married at our home church and again, Papa came to the wedding. Sarah put both her parents' names on the invitation, in spite of an uncle advising her not to put Papa's name on it. At their reception another uncle, shocked to see Papa, spoke angrily to him, "The nerve! You ought to be ashamed to show your face!" It seemed scandalous to him that Papa came to his daughter's wedding!

Relating this incident later, Papa said, "I felt sorry for him; he was so angry."

I found that ironic—that Papa felt sorry for our uncle!

Sarah and John lived in a big city where they participated in the work of a small mission church. The city was located not far from where Papa and Jenny lived. Instead of attending Catholic Church with Jenny, Papa often came to Sarah and John's Mennonite mission church. There, where people did not know much about his life, he joined in worship, sang heartily, and brought paper supplies for the church. He worked at that time for a paper supply company. Then Sarah often invited Papa to her home for Sunday dinner. Papa raved about Sarah's gracious hospitality, her good housekeeping, and wonderful mothering. Sarah and John's five children enjoyed the visits from their Grandpa Johns. He often brought them gifts, and said nice things to encourage them.

Papa seemed to be confident that God had forgiven his past sins. One of the pastors from the city mission church tried to help Papa to be reconciled to the Mennonite church where he was earlier excommunicated because of unethical financial doings. He met with the ministers from the earlier church, but they did not feel comfortable restoring membership for Papa while he still lived with Jenny, even though he claimed he was not any longer living in adultery with her. So the membership was never restored, but Papa kept on in fellowship with the mission church, and later with another Mennonite church in the area where he and Jenny lived.

Like Sarah, all the rest of us enjoyed having Papa present for the important times in our lives. But better yet, we wished for Papa to be back home with Mama so ours would be a normal family.

CHAPTER 8

In the small crowded house in New Jersey, Jenny finished folding the laundry, and went upstairs to put it away. Then with aching back and swollen feet, she sat down to read a book. "I deserve a little rest," she said aloud.

She soon tossed the novel aside. She found it hard to concentrate on anything these days. The last letter from Steve's oldest daughter in Pennsylvania lay open on the table. She picked up the letter and read it again.

> Dear Jenny,
>
> Do you know what a sin it is for you to live with a man who is already married? The Bible says, "For the wages of sin is death, but the gift of God is eternal life." Please confess your sins and change your life so that you can know the second part of that verse.
>
> Sincerely, Beth

She lay the letter aside. *If Beth would only know what I*

have to put up with, she thought. Steve had read it and said, "Don't pay any attention to that. Beth doesn't understand." But that didn't help her forget it.

Jenny's thoughts were soon interrupted by Julie and Angie. Once the girls awoke from their naps, she could no longer read or rest. Four-year-old Julie patted Mama's large tummy. "When will the baby come out, Mommy?" she asked.

"Maybe in a few days," Jenny said.

"Goody, goody! Angie, we're going to have a baby soon," she called to her two year old sister.

"Baby, baby," said Angie.

Jenny wished she could be as happy about it as the girls. But with Steve away so much, and feeling guilty about even living with him, she dreaded trying to raise another child.

When the baby came, however, they named her Susan. As Jenny fed and cared for the new baby, she found herself singing, and almost forgot to be troubled. Susan was a ray of sunshine.

• • • • •

Years later, when they had just moved, Jenny stood in the living room doorway of their "new" home. *A clean start in a new town,* she thought. She wasn't sure when she first knew she needed to change things. Maybe it started at the wedding when her friend, Jane, walked back the aisle holding Jeff's arm, beaming with joy. Maybe it was seeing her cousin and husband celebrating their twentieth anniversary. Or was it when Steve *again* left her and the children alone on Christmas day.

I must tell him. She didn't have the heart to ask him to leave for good. The girls needed a daddy—even if only a part-time daddy. Furthermore, they had bought this house together.

She inhaled deeply, trying to work up enough courage. Her stomach lurched when she thought of how angry and hurt Steve would be.

"Are you all right?" he asked, watching her over the newspaper he was reading.

She almost said, "I'm fine." Instead, she took a few steps into the room and began.

"Steve, I can't do it anymore."

"You can't do what?"

"Can't live the way we're living. I'm making everything right in my church, and will be able to take communion again. In this house we'll sleep in separate rooms. You may sleep in the upstairs bedroom and I'll take the room here on the first floor."

• • • • •

Now it was out. She waited tensely for his response. But as usual, not a word from Steve. Stone-faced, saying nothing, he started taking his clothes up the steps. No fight, no words. Jenny watched him silently.

"I'm sorry," she said. "I know you went through this with Mary. But I need to do it for my own peace of mind." Steve had told her how Mary had put him out of the bedroom after their fourth child was born. He had said Mary was afraid of having more children and felt they could not afford any more.

Poor man, he has two women, but no wife. Tough, but he brought it on himself.

Steve continued his work as a salesman and gave Jenny enough money for the basics, but he came and went as he pleased, not telling her where he was going or when he'd be back. Jenny learned to live with it, but it became more difficult for the girls.

"Why does Daddy always go away on Christmas?" pouted Julie.

What could Jenny say? Julie would not understand that Daddy must take his other family and go to his mother's home for Christmas.

CHAPTER 9

As we children got older, Papa talked more about the children in his second "marriage." He talked about Julie and Angie. But one day I learned that Papa had a third daughter, Susan, in his other family.

It was in 1961, after I had been teaching school for three years, that my cousin, Joe, called me aside at a Johns family reunion.

"You've gotta hear this," he began. "Last week I was at a training seminar in New Jersey and I met a young lady with the name Johns. I told her that my mother was a Johns from Lancaster County.

"She said, 'My father came from Lancaster County. Maybe we are related!'"

"So I asked her what her father's name is, and she said, 'Steve.' And yes, she knew that he had five children in Lancaster. So we knew her father was my Uncle Steve."

"'That makes us cousins!' I said, and reached out for a handshake."

"Wow," I reacted, my heart pounding. "What's her name? What did she look like?"

"Angela Johns. She has reddish-blond hair and she showed me pictures of her older sister, Julie, and her younger sister, Susan."

"What?" I interrupted. "There are three of them? We only ever heard about two, Julia and Angela."

"Well, she showed me the picture of Susan, and she has blond hair and looks like she could very well be your sister. We had fun talking together."

"Wait till I tell my sister, Nancy!"

Later that week I spent the day with Nancy, who was married and lived eight miles away. While her baby, Jan, napped, I told Nancy the story Joe had told me on Sunday.

"Oh no," said Nancy. "So Papa's still not telling us the whole truth. I think I'll ask him about it when he comes up the next time."

"Yes, do that. You get to talk to him more than I do since I still live with Mama, and Papa stays at your house when he comes to visit. I wonder what he'll say."

"Well, you know Papa. He'll have some smooth way to explain it."

• • • • •

Nancy did ask Papa about it the next time he came up. And Nancy hurried to tell me what she learned.

"You remember that time when Papa came home after he had appendicitis?"

"I sure do," I answered. "And I can still feel the hurt when I think about Uncle Jesse coming and taking him away."

"Yes. And Papa says that when he came up on the bus that time he was planning to stay. He said he had made arrangements for Jenny to be taken care of by her brothers and he would not need to go back to her."

"Really? I wonder! Do you think he really meant that?"

"Who knows? That's what he said. And so when Uncle Jesse came and took him back to Jenny, he just gave up and stayed there with Jenny. And it was after that that they had the third child."

"Humm! How does that make you feel?"

"Confused. I don't know what to think."

"That's how I feel, too," I said.

"But that's not all," continued Nancy. "Papa and I got into a deep discussion and he told me a lot of stuff I never knew before. Just wait till you hear this!"

"What? Come on. Tell me everything." I could hardly wait to hear anything that would help untangle the mystery of Papa's life.

"He said that when they lived on the farm, one night he came home and his clothes and things were moved out of Mama's room over into the spare room. This was about a half year after Sarah was born. He didn't think Mama would have done that, but she was afraid of having more children which she thought they could not afford. He says Mama's mother encouraged her to do that."

"Oh no," I groaned. "You know, ... come to think of it, as long as I can remember, every place we lived, Papa always slept in a separate bedroom from Mama. At that time I didn't know anything different and didn't think it strange. And you were too young to remember, or do you?"

"Well, I remember I slept in Mama's bed a lot. I was a real Mama baby. But most of the years when I was old enough to remember, Papa was gone a lot."

"I wonder how it happened that you even came to be."

"Well, I asked Mama that one time. Didn't I ever tell you about that?"

"No, what did she say?"

"She said that she heard a noise in the night and went over and crawled in bed with Papa because she was scared. And then it happened."

"But getting back to what Papa told me," continued Nancy, "he said that when he met Jenny he was so discouraged that he felt like driving into a stone wall to end it all."

"Oh Nancy, did he really say that? Why was he so discouraged? Probably because he was estranged from Mama," I answered my own question.

"Yes, and then when he met Jenny she was such an encouragement to him. He can't see how his relationship with her could be all so bad because she helped him so much. Imagine that!"

"Well," I said. "That's a different picture than we usually get about the whole thing. Maybe Jenny saved Papa's life."

"Papa said he knows that what he did was wrong, but when he was in it he saw no easy way out. He even admitted to me that, as the Bible says, 'The way of the transgressor is hard.'"

"Umm. Maybe we shouldn't be so hard on Papa." I paused and then continued, "But we do love him and pray for him. And we accept him when he comes to visit us. He is our father and he has never been mean to us."

"He's a puzzle. That's what he is!" said Nancy.

"Don't you wonder sometimes," I continued, "what it must be like for his other family? Wouldn't it be kind of interesting if we could meet them sometime?"

CHAPTER 10

As I was about to start the lawn mower, the telephone rang. Another interruption! I did want to get the lawn mowed this morning.

"Hello?"

"Amanda, this is Nancy." Panic sounded in her voice. "Guess what! Papa called this morning and said he is bringing his girls to meet me today. Amanda, you must come and be with me. You know Joy is only two weeks old and I don't feel up to meeting them myself. Can you come?"

"Oh Nancy! How can he do this to us on such short notice? Do you want to meet them?"

"I had no choice. He said he is coming and that they want to meet us. Please come, Amanda. I need your moral support."

"Okay, but what shall I tell Mother? She might not feel good about us seeing them." I quickly glanced around to see if Mother was hearing this, and was relieved to see her outside picking tomatoes.

"Well, tell her I need your help with Joy. She'd understand that. You better not tell Beth either. She might not be able to handle it right now."

"That might work. What time must I be there?"

"Just come as soon as you can."

• • • • •

So I put the lawn mower away and got dressed to go. I had only three weeks left before school started. I wanted to do some planning and studying after I finished the lawn. But I willingly changed my plans for Nancy's sake. And besides I was curious to see what my half sisters were like.

Mother didn't seem to care that I went to help Nancy, and fortunately did not ask to go along. She had been with Nancy for several days after she and the baby had come from the hospital. Besides, she was in the middle of canning tomato juice.

So I drove alone the ten miles to Nancy's home, my hands sweating as I gripped the steering wheel. My mind raced over events of the past—I remembered the time ten years ago when I learned that there were three half sisters instead of two. At that time, Mother, Beth, and I, still lived in the large house along the busy highway. The house by the stream and the big garden made a lot of work and with my teaching, and Beth working full time at the bookstore, it seemed a good time to lighten the burden for Mama and move to a smaller place. So two years ago, we had sold the place and Beth and I bought a three bedroom rancher in a town away from the highway.

I arrived in time to eat lunch with Nancy and the girls. I loved being with my nieces, Jan and Jolyn, and now baby Joy.

Then we waited. As usual we didn't know exactly when Papa would come. We talked about the times when we were children and used to chant, "Papa, Papa, do come. Papa, Papa, do come."

Papa still came to visit his grown children in Pennsylvania, Maryland, and Ohio. Papa often stayed overnight at Nancy and Tom's house and then drove the ten miles to visit Beth, Mama, and me. Both Andy and Sarah lived out of state, so Papa's visit to Nancy was not unusual. But now Papa wanted us to meet the children of his other woman! *That* was something else. He had told each family only a little about the other.

• • • • •

"Do you think they will look like us? What will we say?" asked Nancy as she paced the floor, glancing out the window.

• • • • •

"Well," I said, as the knot in my stomach got tighter, "we need have nothing against them. They can't help it that they were . . . I was about to say illegitimate. But that's not fair. It is really the parents that are illegitimate. So we might as well accept them."

"Sure, that's right," agreed Nancy. "Look here they come."

As usual Papa drove a shiny new car, and wore a dress suit, tie, and white shoes.

"Amanda, they're getting out. They are really nice looking." She grabbed my arm for security. "Shall we go out and welcome them?"

"Hi Papa," Nancy and I greeted him.

"Hi, how are you? This is Angie Williams, this is Julie Kline, and then here is Susan Johnson." Papa never called them his daughters and emphasized their married names.

"Hi! I'm Nancy, and this is Amanda. Come on in," said Nancy. "Joy is sleeping, but you can take a peek at her. She is only two weeks old. And these are my daughters, Jan and Jolyn. Jan is ten and Jolyn is eight."

After a few minutes of uneasiness, the five of us got to chatting as if we had known each other for years. We talked about their children, jobs, and travels, and about ours. We discussed similarities and differences in our appearances. Susan had blond hair like mine. Julie, like me, seemed to be the spokesperson for her siblings. But we all talked and in a short time knew that we liked each other.

Papa wanted to take some pictures, but discovered his film was full. So he quickly left to go get a new film. Wow! Little did he know what a "mistake" he made when he left us girls to ourselves. We got to sharing things we did not feel free to say in Papa's presence.

I wanted to know how old Julie was.

"I'm 29. I'm married and have three children. How old are you?" asked Julie.

"I'm 40. I am single and live with my mother and my older sister Beth. Beth is single, too, and works in a bookstore. I've been teaching school for thirteen years.

"How old are you, Nancy? You're the youngest, aren't' you? asked Julie.

"Yes, I'm the baby. I'm 32."

"Umm. Looks like by the ages we could be one continuous family. Right?" volunteered Angie. "I am just two years younger than Julie, and Susan is two years younger than I."

"So," I observed, "there are only three years between the two families."

"What we can't understand," said Julie as she walked across the room to look more closely at the family photo on the wall, "is why we can't go to see our grandmother Johns. Daddy says his people are Mennonites and because we are Catholics they wouldn't want to meet us."

"Oh, no," I exclaimed. "That is not true. Did Papa say that? We are Mennonites, but that doesn't mean we don't associate with other people."

"Really? Then why can't we meet them?" continued Julie. She turned and faced me.

"Well," I hesitated, "Grandma is upset with Papa because he left his wife and lived with another woman. I think it would pain her to see you. It would make the whole thing seem too real. He comes to visit her with *us*, and perhaps she would rather deny the reality of the situation. I don't know."

"On the other hand," said Nancy, "I doubt Papa has asked her if she wanted to meet you. He keeps his two families separate. He really respects his mother and probably is afraid of hurting her. So he pretends to her like he belongs to us. He is her oldest son, and you might say he was Mama's pet. She can scarcely believe the kind of life he is living.

"But when someone is divorced," began Angie as she leaned forward in her chair.

"Oh, but our parents were never divorced," I quickly corrected. "But that wouldn't make much difference to Grandma. Mennonites believe that divorce is wrong."

"You say they were never divorced?" Angie asked.

"That's right," agreed Nancy. "Mama never wanted a divorce. She says she promised to be true to Papa for life. She treats him kindly when he comes even after all that happened."

"And besides," I added, "Papa never asked her for a divorce."

Angie, Julie and Susan looked at each other in disbelief.

And then Nancy came out with it. She started walking toward the cradle to pick up Joy. "Well, do you know if your parents were ever married?"

"Ever married, why of course, well, ... uh, ... uh, ..."

They all three seemed so shocked that Nancy and I felt like maybe we had said too much. We didn't mean to be telling them something they didn't already know.

After a tense silence, Julie, with determination in her voice, said, "I'm going to find out."

We quickly changed the subject as Papa came in with the film. We all gathered around Nancy and Joy and started oohing and ahing over the pretty baby. Papa took pictures of the baby, Jan and Jolyn, and then of all five sisters together.

Papa appeared unaware of the emotional trauma the meeting of his daughters had caused, but he couldn't sit still long and soon announced it was time to leave.

"I want to take the girls to see the farm where I grew up," he said. "There we'll see my brother and his family."

But take them to see his mother? He never even mentioned it as a possibility.

As they got up to leave, Papa didn't seem to notice the silence of Angie, Julie and Susan. Nancy and I gave each of the girls a big sisterly hug, and I noticed tears in Angie's eyes.

The bond we established between us that day proved to be a permanent one. We knew this would not be the end of our visits with each other.

CHAPTER 11

Only a few weeks went by before I got a call from Julie. She wanted to come, without Papa this time, and also without Angie and Susan, to talk more with Nancy and me. We agreed to meet at a restaurant near my home and have lunch together.

I again felt pressure to get ready to teach. But my eagerness to talk more with Julie won out for my time on that Labor Day Monday in 1971 when school started the next day. I had never told Mama about meeting Papa's other daughters. I had confided in Beth and Sarah. Andy lived in Ohio with his wife and children, and I had not had an opportunity to talk to him about it.

At the restaurant the three of us greeted each other with hugs and sensed a kindred spirit from the start. It wasn't long until we were chatting away. But soon Julie got to the point of what she wanted to tell us.

"After our trip to Pennsylvania, I did some detective work to find out if Mama and Daddy were ever married," began Julie. "I could hardly wait to find out the truth. I checked first with Aunt Alice. She said it was possible that they were not married. No one else seemed to know for sure, so I decided I must confront them directly. I went over to the house and Daddy was outside on a ladder painting the house. So I approached Mama first."

"'Mama,' I said. 'Tell me about your wedding. When did you marry? Did you have a church wedding?'"

"'Why do you ask that?' she replied after a moment's pause."

"'Okay, I might as well tell you the whole story. Daddy took us up to Pennsylvania and we met two of our half sisters.'"

"'Yes, I know. Your Daddy told me about it. So what happened?'"

"'We asked them why we couldn't visit our grandmother,' I continued, 'and they said their grandmother was upset because Daddy had left their mother for another woman and that they were not divorced. Then they asked us if our parents were ever married. They thought you and Daddy were living together without being married. Is that true?'"

"Her quick reply was, 'Go ask your Daddy about that.' But after a moment's pause she continued, 'Whatever happened was because of the lies your father told me.'"

"Then I knew you guys were probably right. And I can't believe that I never asked them before. Somehow my parents always knew how to change the subject from something they did not wish to tell us. But now I was determined to know the whole truth."

"So I marched right out to Daddy. I called to him up there on the ladder. I said, 'Daddy, come down here. I need to talk to you.'"

"'What's the matter?' he asked. 'Can't I finish this panel before I come down?'"

"'No,' I said. 'I need to ask you something *right* now.'"

"So he slowly came down and eyed me with a sheepish look. He appeared to sense that I had something to say that he didn't wish to hear."

"I put the question to him abruptly. 'Daddy, were you and Mama ever married?'"

"Whew. It was out. I waited for the answer. Just like Mama, he said, 'Why do you ask that?'"

"So I told him what you all said while he was out for the film. He didn't respond right away, but neither did he get angry."

"I persisted, 'Well, are you married?'"

"'Not to your mother,' he said."

"We both sat down on the grass and then he talked."

"'No,' he continued, 'we were not married. But we couldn't tell your mother's mother that, so we pretended to be married. And your grandmother accepted us.' He told me about how discouraged he was about how things were going with your mother, and how he met my mother. He said my mother was young and free, and we should not blame her."

"Actually, I think he was relieved that the truth was out."

"Oh, Julie, how does this make you feel?" I asked.

"Mixed up." she answered. "I shared it all with Angie and Susan, and we all three went through a traumatic time with emotions ranging from anger to pity. We said, 'So we're illegitimates.'"

"But you are not," I countered. "A child is never illegitimate. It is the parents who are illegitimate. You had no say in the matter of your birth. God loves you. He loves your parents, too, and will forgive them if they are sorry."

"Humm, well maybe they are sorry. I don't know. I really feel mixed up about it. I love them both, and yet I feel angry. But we're learning to live with it. What else can we do?"

"That's the way with us," said Nancy. "We're learning to live with it. We know that God loves us. We know we have to forgive our father for what he has done. That isn't easy. Sometimes we are not sure if we have forgiven him. And we can see some good in it. For one thing , we get to meet you!"

"That's right," I agreed. "It's fun learning to know our half sisters. Tell us more about your life."

We talked on until the agreed-upon time for the lunch visit to end. All too soon, Julie needed to be on her way.

We agreed to meet again soon and learn more about our father, who is Papa to one family and Daddy to the other.

CHAPTER 12

In the fall of 1972, I telephoned Papa. "Will you be able to take us to Ohio to visit Andy's family over Thanksgiving again this year? I get off from school at noon on Wednesday, and Beth can take off then, too. I'll need to be back for school on Monday."

"Sure," came Papa's cheerful answer. "I'll come up on Wednesday morning, and we can get out there by evening like we did last year, although the turnpike might be crowded the night before the holiday. I'm eager to see Andy. I have a bicycle for Lamar. I hope we can get everything in the car."

"Good. We'll try to pack lightly, although Mama always wants to take lots of food you know. I'll call Andy and Esther, but I'm sure it will be fine with them."

This was getting to be an annual thing—a Thanksgiving trip to Ohio—Papa and Mama with Beth and me.

When the day came for us to start out, we packed our

luggage and the food Mama had prepared into Papa's shiny Buick. The sun shone brightly as we headed west from Lancaster toward the turnpike. When we traveled together, I always sat up front with Papa, while Beth rode in the back seat with Mama. It was not quite so awkward for Mama that way. We sang a lot on those trips. Beth knew many hymns and choruses from memory, and Papa joined in on a lot of them. This and our lighthearted chatter helped lessen the tension for Mama. Some of the time Papa asked me to drive. I enjoyed driving.

After seven hours of travel, we pulled into Andy's lane. As soon as they saw us, tousled boys and schoolgirls spilled out of the house, bubbling with excitement. Esther scurried down the steps drying her hands on her apron as she approached, and Andy swung through the garage side door almost running. We had one grand reunion with warm hugs enjoyed in abundance. Even the boys submitted to being kissed by Grandma and Grandpa and the aunts.

"My, Ruth, how tall you've grown," Beth laughed as she hugged her.

"And look what long braids Elaine has by now," exclaimed Mama.

"How did you like school this year?" I asked Ann, as she took my bag to accompany me into the house. I had to lean close to her to hear her reply because by now everyone seemed to be talking at once.

"What color will you paint this Chevy?" Papa asked Andy about the car he was fixing in his spare time.

"It looks like someone painted the porch," Beth said approvingly as she climbed the steps.

"Guess what, Grandpa," Lamar shouted above the others. "I got a prize in school for ..." his voice got lost in the crowd.

After the initial commotion had subsided somewhat, we all sat down at the table for a late evening supper of Esther's homemade chili, cornbread, pickles, German Chocolate cake, and ice cream. When seated at the table Papa always sat beside Mama, and both seemed cheerful. An onlooker might think they were a normal married couple.

Papa tried one of his riddles on five-year-old Wade. "What's black and white and red all over?" he asked.

When Wade didn't answer right away, Papa answered, "The newspaper is black and white and read all over the world!"

The others joined him in a hearty chuckle.

Over the next few days, Papa took care to give each member of Andy's family some special attention. He had brought a yellow youth-sized bicycle along for Lamar. He also took Ruth and Ann on a bicycle ride to the neighbors. Papa rode bike regularly for his health. He told Ruth and her father about a small boy who had ridiculed him for riding bike. This boy thought it odd to see a Grandpa riding bike on the sidewalk. Papa told them how he solved the problem. "I found a second-hand bike that fit him wonderfully and now he is my friend," he finished.

"Isn't that just like Papa?" I whispered to Andy. "I think that's not the first bike he's given away."

On Thursday morning Mama worked in the kitchen all morning with Esther. Following her own tradition for their Thanksgiving visits, she roasted a turkey with stuffing and the works. She had baked shoofly and pumpkin pies in Pennsylvania before we traveled.

"Does she try extra hard to fix some of Papa's favorite foods to show him she still loves him?" I wondered.

While Beth and Esther and Mama prepared dinner, I took the chance to enjoy my nieces and nephews. "Look, I brought a new book to read to you," I offered. "Who wants to join us?" Four or five children soon snuggled near me while I introduced them to E.B. White's *Charlotte's Web,* a favorite of mine. I often read it to my second graders at school.

After breakfast Papa had put on his paint-spattered blue coveralls and set up a ladder to paint the front of the house. Last year he had painted a back section. He liked to be useful when he visited Andy.

Everyone gladly stopped what they were doing when the call came for dinner. We all sang together "Praise God from Whom All Blessings Flow" before Andy led in prayer for the meal. While everyone was busy eating, there was a time of silence, but soon the chatter, stories and jokes continued between bites of the delicious dinner.

After dinner, the girls sang together as they washed dishes. Ruth, Ann, and Elaine, sang in beautiful three-part harmony. Papa was painting the siding just outside the kitchen window. Through the open window he called, "I really like that song. I love to hear my granddaughters sing. It makes me feel so happy." (Papa never passed up an opportunity to give a compliment.)

The girls blushed with pleasure. But Ruth whispered to me, "I wonder what he really thinks when we sing songs of Heaven. Oh, how I wish he would live at Grandma's house again!" Andy had earlier explained to Ruth and Ann, the two oldest girls, why Grandpa lived in New Jersey. The younger children did not realize that Grandpa and Grandma did not live together. Ruth and Ann told me they prayed nightly that God would "bring Grandpa and Grandma back together again.

That evening most of us attended a revival meeting at Andy's home church. Papa went, too. The Holy Spirit moved in the hearts of the listeners. When opportunity was given for testimonies, Ruth was one of several youth who responded with a spoken "word for the Lord."

Later that evening, around the table with popcorn and tea, I was surprised to hear Papa say, "It made me very happy to hear my granddaughter give her testimony tonight." Then looking directly at Ruth, he finished, "Keep right on in the path you are going."

As Ruth discussed this with me later, she said this was a moment she would never forget. "Did Grandpa wish he could go back and do things differently?" This was a question she could not ask. Andy's family never talked to Grandpa about his "other family" and he never talked about the matter to them.

On Friday, Papa again painted, and the rest of us worked at various things, but I also had time to go shopping with the children. I enjoyed buying things for them.

On Saturday afternoon, everyone stopped work early and we got together outside under a shade tree and sang. There were trio numbers, school program songs for Grandma and Grandpa, and songs for everyone. We always sang "My Jesus I love Thee" at Grandpa's request and his strong voice boomed louder than anyone else's.

Sunday afternoon we headed back to Pennsylvania filled with warm memories of a happy weekend. Some of the children had cried as we hugged them goodbye. They all loved when we visited them. And I realized that my Papa was their beloved Grandpa.

CHAPTER 13

I enjoyed teaching second grade at the local public school, but a change looked good to me when I met Phil. We met at a summer camp where I served as a counselor and Phil taught nature and Bible classes. He had returned home from overseas mission work two years earlier. Phil and I got acquainted in the informal atmosphere of the camp and it didn't take long for me to realize that I thought of Phil as more than a casual friend. I didn't know if Phil shared my feeling about it until several months later when he wrote and asked if I would like to correspond and get better acquainted.

In spite of the unfaithfulness of my father, I was not averse to having a male friendship, and hoped to marry sometime. During a six-month courtship, Phil and I discussed many things. After much prayer, and a great sense of peace that it was the right thing to do, I answered yes to Phil's proposal for marriage.

Soon we began making wedding plans. Our wedding took place at my home church. Again, Papa came for my special occasion, and I was happy to have him there. My brother Andy and his wife sang a duet, which began "Since first my soul was knit to thine." My sister-in-law from my husband's family, led a chorus of our nieces and nephews. We enjoyed having our two families unite on our special day. Phil had been married before and his wife had died. His son and daughter stood with us as attendants, and his son gave a beautiful welcome to both families. I wore a simple white street-length dress and my usual white prayer veiling, and carried one red rose. Phil wore a plain suit. What we call a plain suit is almost like a Nehru jacket, with no layback collar. My pastor married us and a good friend of Phil's preached the sermon. After the ceremony we stood near the exit and friends and relatives greeted us.

Then we went to the church basement, where the church's trustees prepared and served a delicious hot meal to us and our 200 guests.

For our honeymoon, we traveled in the New England states.

We found a house for sale that seemed to be God's perfect answer, located near enough for me to travel the ten miles to my school and for Phil to drive the four miles to his work.

At the public auction, I bid on and bought the house, as Phil was out of town for a church meeting.

Now that I had a home away from my mother, Papa often stayed at my house when he came to visit family. Papa liked Phil. He told me, "I think Phil is the best thing that ever happened to you. Right?"

"Yes, next to knowing Jesus as my Savior, Phil is probably the best thing that ever happened to me," I answered.

When Papa came to visit us, as usual, he wore a suit and tie, and drove a nice car, although not such a late model as he used to drive when he sold cars. He kept the car clean and polished so that it looked almost new. Now Phil didn't value a clean car like Papa did. Papa didn't criticize Phil for that, but offered, "May I wash your car for you, Amanda?"

"Sure, Papa, I'd like that," I said. So Papa dressed in his suit and tie, often shined up Phil's VW Beetle and my American Motors Matador. He brought me a really nice brush to use for washing the car. I use that often and think of Papa. My siblings each have a brush like that from Papa. Often he mowed lawn for us, too. And yes, even that he did wearing long-sleeved shirt and tie! I never saw my father wearing blue jeans and tee shirt.

Papa continued his salesman job at a supply company in New Jersey. He often brought paper napkins, paper towels, toilet tissue, and Kleenex for us. Of course, Papa also often ate meals at our house. Many times I'd forget to put napkins on the table, and Papa held up his hands and wiggled his fingers saying, "Do you have a napkin or something?" Then I quickly brought out napkins. This got to be kind of a family joke, because he supplied us all with napkins, and yet he had to ask for one at my house!

During these visits with Phil and me, Papa talked more about Jenny and his three daughters in New Jersey. I still believed that Papa was living in adultery, but he tried to explain. "Yes, we are living in the same house, but ever since about twelve years ago Jenny and I are not living as husband and wife. I knew that was wrong, so I moved to a bedroom upstairs. You can live that way when you are older."

Phil and I didn't know if we should believe that or not, until we got the story from Angie and Julie.

CHAPTER 14

One day my half sister, Angie, called me and said, "I'd like to host a dinner party at my house with you and Phil. My two sisters and their husbands will be here. I'd also like to have Nancy and Sarah and their husbands. Could you and Phil come?"

"Oh, Angie, we'd love to come. Yes, I think next Saturday would suit us. Thank you. It would be great to get together again, and also to meet your husbands. You never met Sarah, did you?"

"No. Do you think she would like to come?"

"Oh, surely!"

• • • • •

We went with some anxiety, thinking, "What will we talk about? What kind of a home will we find out Angie lived in?" But when we arrived, our fears dissolved and we soon sensed that special sisterly bonding we knew when we first met our half sisters.

"Hi Angie," I greeted her with a big hug. Many hugs rounded out the warm greetings as we all met—Angie and Herb, Julie and George, Susan and Joel, from Papa's second family, together with Sarah and John, Nancy and Tom, and Phil and I from Papa's first family.

Angie, who hosted the party, did not invite Papa. She said, "I wanted to be able to talk with all of you and learn more about Daddy and his family."

I wasn't sure who learned the most by the time the evening was over.

"Oh, you have a beautiful home, Angie." We all oohed and aahed as we toured the garden, lawn, and house, then gathered for dinner on the deck. After raving over the food, we settled into the conversation all had been eagerly waiting for.

"You know," began Julie, her fork holding a meatball, "we really don't have fond childhood memories of Daddy. He came and went and lots of times we didn't know where he was, especially for important holidays, like Christmas."

"Umm." That surprised me. I stopped eating and looked at Julie. "We thought he left us and lived with you. You had our Papa. But it sounds like you didn't really have him either."

"We were especially sad, and even angry at Christmas," continued Julie. "He always packed his little suitcase on Christmas Eve and left. 'I'm going to Pennsylvania to my mother for the family Christmas dinner,' he explained. We knew it would do no good to beg him to stay. So we watched him go, and then turned around to Mama for comfort. She was our Christmas angel."

"We told you," Angie took up the story, "that he told us our Grandmother Johns was Mennonite and wouldn't want to see us because we are Catholic. Now we know that's not true, but back then we didn't know better. When I asked Daddy why he didn't take us to see our grandmother, he said, 'Why do you want to meet her if she doesn't want to meet you?' I carried this sadness with me for a long time. However, I never thought of my unknown grandmother as a harsh woman. It just made me sad that Daddy told me that. I always thought I was a lovable little girl and that if my grandma met me she would love me."

Then Nancy joined in the conversation. "Is it true, as Papa tells us, that he and your mother don't sleep together anymore? Papa says he knew it was wrong and that when you are older you can live that way. He sometimes referred to your mother as his domestic engineer. Do they really live separate like that?"

"Yes, that is absolutely true," spoke up Julie. "They do sleep in separate bedrooms for some years now. But his reason is not true. You can't believe everything he tells you."

Sarah kept quiet up to this time, but now she laid down her spoon and shyly asked, "What do you mean about his reason not being true?"

Julie paused before answering as Angie brought out the dessert, and for a bit all eyes focused on the beautifully decorated cake.

"Did you make it?" I asked.

"Guess what! My husband, Herb, baked it," said Angie, "and I decorated it."

"Wow, its lovely," said Nancy. "It is really great of you to make this meal for all of us. Wouldn't Papa be surprised if he knew what all we are learning about him?"

"Well, he deserves it, after all the lies he told us over the years," said Julie. "Now back to the question. Yes, they do sleep in separate rooms. But that was not his choice. Mama made that decision."

"Really?" That answer shed a different light on Papa's situation. Everyone was silent for some minutes as they ate cake and ice cream and pondered this bit of news.

"Yes," Angie took up the story. "Mama got tired of feeling guilty and being barred from communion in the church, so she confessed to the priest. When the priest told her she would no longer be living in sin if they did not live as husband and wife, she demanded that Daddy take the room upstairs. It was *Mama's* decision, not Daddy's."

"We wonder," Julie continued, "why our mother kept living with Daddy. They didn't have a compatible relationship. Communication between them was almost nil there for a while."

"Poor Daddy! He didn't seem to have much backbone. Didn't your mother put him out of the bedroom, too? Why didn't he stand up for his rights? Seems to me like he was kind of chicken," concluded Angie.

"I can hardly believe we're talking like this," added Susan. "Everything Angie and Julie said is absolutely true. And yet," she paused before continuing. "And yet, we still love Daddy."

"Yes, we do," echoed all the sisters.

Later in the conversation Julie posed the question, "How did we all turn out to be such nice people?"

That started a big round of discussion.

"Our mother is really a nice person," said Susan. "You all should come and meet her sometime. And I'd like to meet your mother."

"Papa has often invited us to come to his house and meet your mother," said Nan. "Maybe we will do it."

"Back to your question, Julie, our church family, and our aunts and uncles influenced us a lot, and they helped us financially, too," I said.

"Also," added Sarah, "Mother and lots of other people prayed for us."

"We had relatives, too, and many friends along the way to help us," said Angie.

"Another thing," began Sarah, "about why we are such nice people, Papa had a lot of good points, too. To be fair shouldn't we give him credit for helping us be nice people?

"Indeed," I continued. "Papa encouraged us in many ways, and it seems he always knows how to say something to make you feel good."

"Yes, that's right." said Nancy. "And he's a people person, can talk to anyone in a friendly way. He's also generous."

"Besides, he's good looking, has a great singing voice, and is always neatly dressed," added Susan.

"Yes," agreed Angie, "we do have some good genes from the Johns family. However, it seems like your part of his family see the good points about him a little more than we do. We did not see him as being generous when we were children. More recently, yes, like when he is eating out with someone he pays the bill and leaves a generous tip."

"And he brings us gifts. All five of us got watches from him for graduation." I added.

Then Nancy spoke up. "And didn't all of you enjoy his tours of Washington? He was an excellent tour guide. He took us to the nicest restaurant and paid our meals. In his sales work he made deliveries to many hotels and government buildings. 'Gobment' buildings, he called them. Remember?

"Yeah, that's what he always called them," we all remembered.

"He was very 'in charge,' Nancy continued, "and knew his way around and how to get into the White House and Capitol and all. It was really fun having Papa as our tour guide. He knew lots of people, too, and greeted them by name. They responded in kind."

After supper Angie got out some hymnbooks and we started singing together. My sisters and I often sang together, but now we learned that our half sisters also like to sing.

"We often sang with our mother. And of course, Daddy likes to sing, too," said Angie. "Do you know this song, 'My Jesus I Love Thee'? It was Daddy's favorite song. We know the tune. Daddy often played it on the piano, but we never learned the words."

As we sang, the words took on new meaning and it seemed ironic to me that Papa loved to sing, "For thee all the follies of sin I resign."

"You know another song Papa often played on the piano?"

"Yes, Sarah," I continued. "He played, 'Oh happy is the man who hears instructions warning voice.' And remember how that irked Mama? She didn't think he was listening well to 'instructions warning voice.'"

Sarah continued, "He often plays that when he comes to my house, too. And I wonder about it."

Nancy added, "Well, did you know that he only knows how to play in one key, and that song is in two sharps. When he plays other songs, he plays them as if they were written in two sharps."

The evening ended with laughing, joking and everybody hugging each other. We all thanked Angie and Herb for the delicious dinner and the fun evening. Everyone agreed, "We must do this again."

• • • • •

On the way home Phil and I discussed the things we learned about Papa. We also talked about our half sisters. "They live in a nice house. It appears to me they live a bit higher on the social scale than we do. I really like them."

After a time of silence I asked Phil, "Do you think Papa really means what he sings? Why is 'My Jesus I Love Thee' his favorite song?"

"Well," said Phil, "maybe your Papa is sorry for his sinful life. You know he told Nancy, 'The way of the transgressor is hard.' Maybe he is sorry for his past sins. No sin is too big for God to forgive, you know. And Amanda, even though they say it was their mother's decision that they sleep in separate bedrooms, I think your Papa may have been relieved, knowing, as he did, that the way he lived was wrong."

"I think you may be right. I hope so," I said, "but I wish we knew for certain that Papa is forgiven."

I found it consoling to be able to discuss my concerns with Phil.

CHAPTER 15

When Jenny arrived from her work at the store, she found Steve already home. She didn't think that too unusual, as he often finished early on Friday. As he walked back and forth in the living room, he bit his lower lip and kept looking out the window.

"What's making you so nervous?" Jenny asked.

"Never mind. I'm okay. I see it's starting to snow. Oh, here they come now."

"Here who comes?"

"Nancy and her family. They were visiting friends in southern New Jersey and are on their way home to Pennsylvania. I invited them to stop in for supper. I wanted them to meet you."

"Well, great! You could have checked with me to see if it suited, or at least told me they were coming. I don't appreciate this kind of surprise!"

As Jenny finished her sentence, Steve was already going out to greet Nancy, Tom, and the three girls.

Jenny watched frantically from the window. They seemed to hesitate to get out of the car. But Steve was motioning for them to come on in. They must have been asking if he was sure it was okay.

Jenny watched them get out of the car. *So that's Nancy! I've heard a lot about her. She's the youngest of his five, I think.* As they came across the porch to the front door, Jenny felt her heart racing. She thought about the letter she had received from Steve's oldest daughter, and knew that they all considered her the big sinner. But Jenny decided to hide her anger at Steve and make the best of the situation.

Steve introduced his youngest daughter, Nancy and her husband, Tom, and their children, Jan, Jolyn and Joy, to Jenny, but he didn't introduce Jenny to them. Apparently they were to assume her identity.

Nancy talked with Jenny, and soon they all relaxed and enjoyed the evening. Jenny brought out a super meal on this short notice. She found some fresh meat in the refrigerator, which apparently Steve had brought home that day. She got some vegetables out of the freezer, and cooked rice. Steve always kept ice cream on hand, which made an easy dessert.

Jenny and Steve didn't talk to each other during the visit, except she ordered, "Steve, we need chairs at the table."

But to Nancy and Tom, Jenny was as friendly as could be, and generous.

After Jenny cleared the table, and Nancy helped wash the dishes, they sat in the living room looking at pictures. Steve proudly showed photos of his "other family." Jenny even got out some toys for the little girls.

As they got up to leave, Tom noticed that it was snowing hard. "Wow! Look at that snow!"

They all rushed to the window. Steve said, "I don't like to see you start out in this. Why don't you stay here overnight?"

He glanced at Jenny as she turned and spoke to Nancy.

"Yes, you'd better stay here. It doesn't look good for traveling."

The snow was already covering the road, and Tom admitted that he didn't relish driving three hours on icy roads after dark.

"Are you sure you have room for us all to sleep here?" Nancy asked.

Well, we'll make room," Jenny said.

So Steve opened up the sleep sofa, Jenny brought out sheets and blankets. Floor beds satisfied the girls, and before long they settled down for the night.

Steve retired to his upstairs room without saying a word to Jenny. Jenny went into her room next to the living room. Pleased with herself for showing hospitality to Steve's "other family," she plopped down on the bed with a big sigh. It didn't appear that Nancy hated her after all.

In the morning after Jenny served her company a breakfast of bacon and cheese casserole, fruit salad which Steve prepared, and hot chocolate, Nancy and Tom gathered their things and started out the door.

"Thanks so much for everything," Nancy began. Then she gave Jenny a big hug, after which Jenny hugged each of the girls.

"Come again," Jenny invited. "I'm so glad I learned to know you."

Steve and Jenny stood on the porch waving "Goodbye" until the car was out of sight.

"Next time, let me know when you invite company, will you?" Jenny asked.

CHAPTER 16

At the age of 89, Papa had an accident which radically changed his way of life. He fell down the steps in his home in New Jersey and broke his neck. His recovery was phenomenal; doctors considered it most unusual for a person his age to recover from this kind of injury. After a long hospital stay, he transferred to a retirement home along with Jenny, who was experiencing memory loss. From that time on, Papa was not allowed to drive. Some of us from both his families met in the retirement home to celebrate Papa's 90th birthday. He was beginning to be forgetful, and we saw at that time that Jenny had regressed quite a bit.

• • • • •

Papa had been attending Pastor John's Mennonite church for many years and when he and Jenny moved to the retirement community and he could no longer drive, someone from the church stopped for him each Sunday. Pastor John, husband of Mama's niece, had questioned Uncle Steve, as he called Papa, about his relationship with God and how things stood between him and Mary and her children.

One Sunday evening Pastor John visited Phil and me, and told us, "I asked Uncle Steve about his relationship with Mary. He seemed unsure about it. I asked him if he would like me to help him get things straightened out. He agreed to a meeting with the family to ask forgiveness of each one of you five children. He said he had told Mary he was sorry, but he felt he needed to forgive her. So he wrote a card telling her that he forgives her."

"Yes," I said. "Mama showed me that card. It seemed strange to me. I thought he should ask her to forgive him. But then, of course, she admitted that she did not always do right by Papa. So it is good that he can forgive her."

"Do you think your mother has forgiven him?" asked Pastor John.

"She says she has, but sometimes I can see some bitterness coming through. It's hard for me to imagine how difficult this is for Mother. I think she has forgiven him, though."

"Well, do you want to arrange a meeting with your mother and all five of you children, for Uncle Steve's sake? Will each of you be willing to tell your father that you forgive him?"

"Yes, I think we can do that. It will be good not only for Papa, but for us, too. We want to forgive him, and are not sure sometimes if we really have. Telling him so is probably a good thing to do."

My siblings all welcomed the opportunity for a reconciliation meeting with Papa. So we all met together on the lawn at Nancy and Tom's.

• • • • •

The majestic oaks provided shade on that hot July afternoon, as our family anxiously awaited the arrival of Papa. Papa didn't come driving his own well polished car as he used to do, but he came as a passenger in Pastor John's car. I wasn't sure who was more nervous—Papa or the five of us.

Papa sat next to Pastor John, immaculately dressed as usual, with suit and tie and his favorite old white shoes. The rest of the family sat in a large circle. Pastor John wisely mediated. Papa addressed the oldest first. "You've always been a good girl; what can I say? I'm sorry for the hardship I caused you, Beth."

"Well, I survived, but I did go through hard times. I quit school early, you know, to help earn money for the family. As a child, I had the privilege of knowing you since I was the oldest, and you spent more time with me than you did with the younger ones. So it was probably harder for me to see you gone from us so much of the time. But I held onto God through it all, and I can sincerely say, I forgive you." Beth finished, as tears welled up in her eyes.

Next Papa spoke to Andy. "Andy and I always got along well. I am proud of you, son, Papa began."

Andy hung his head in silence till, with a little prodding from Pastor John, Papa came out with, "Can you forgive me?"

Andy looked up at Papa. "The hardest part for me was not having a father around to teach me how to be a man. I think I could have learned how to be a better husband and father to my family if I had lived with a father who set a good example for me. However, my faith in God helped me, and like Beth, I survived, and…" after a pause, "I forgive you."

It appeared difficult for Papa to admit he had hurt any of his children. He was so used to saying nice things to people and about people. But Pastor John knew how to keep nudging him along.

Next came my turn.

"I've always had a good relationship with Amanda," he began.

I went over and stood beside him, and my voice shook as I spoke, "I love you Papa, but I need to say, too, that I forgive you for times when you disappointed me—when you weren't there for me." I leaned over and gave Papa a gentle hug, and Papa kissed me.

When it came Sarah's turn, she couldn't speak for crying. Papa again said complimentary things about Sarah. He had often visited in her home and praised her as a wonderful housewife and mother.

With a little more help from Pastor John, "Uncle Steve, you know why we called this meeting."

Then, "I'm sorry," was all Papa said.

And between sobs Sarah replied with, "I forgive you." And after a pause, "I love you, Papa."

Nancy, the youngest, didn't give Papa time to say all the nice stuff. Instead of crying, she appeared to be struggling with anger. She was quite young when Papa left Mama. She made it clear to him, "I grew up without a father."

Papa squirmed, put his hand to his head, and after a pause, spoke brokenly, "I'm sorry, Nancy. Please forgive me."

Nancy softened. She put her hand on Papa's and said. "I love you, Papa, and I forgive you."

Up to this point Mama just sat there without saying a word. Pastor John said, "Now, Uncle Steve, what do you want to say to Mary?"

Both nearing ninety years of age, were somewhat frail, and remained seated opposite each other in the circle. Papa looked at Mama, and began, "I am sorry for the way things went and I forgive you and hope you can forgive me."

Slowly, but clearly, Mama spoke, "Thank you. I'm sorry, too. If I had known back at the beginning what I learned since then, I think our life together could have been different. I regret that I did not do my part as your wife. I'm glad you can forgive me, and I do forgive you, too."

To conclude the meeting, Pastor John prayed for Papa and Mama and all us children. It was a good meeting, and everyone breathed a sigh of relief. Then we started reminiscing and shared laughter as well as tears. Sarah remembered, "I had to go door to door and sell things to help Mama make ends meet, and I hated to do that."

"I didn't mind selling when people stopped at the house for things, but I didn't like going from door to door either," I added.

Then we got to talking about things we remembered Papa saying.

"Remember, Papa, what you used to say after we served you a good meal? You said, 'That will do 'till we eat right."

Papa giggled. "Yeah, I did say that, didn't I?"

"Yes," Sarah recalled, "And you used to say, 'The meal is only as good as the pie and ice cream that follow.'"

"And then I'd say," Papa took up the memories, "I've had elegant sufficiency. More would be superfluous redundancy.

And if you had the idosity to doubt my veracity, you have a most pugnacious personality." This brought a big laugh as we all remembered this saying.

"But in these later years," said Beth, "you had a new tune. You said, 'It takes me longer to rest than to get tired.'"

"You can say that again;" Papa responded. "That's the way it is now."

Nancy brought out light refreshments, and we all sang a few songs together. Papa and Mama both sang along heartily, "My Jesus I Love Thee."

Soon Pastor John and Papa departed. (I learned later from Pastor John that on their way home Papa thanked him again and again for arranging this meeting.)

• • • • •

We five siblings often discussed the meeting. We realized it took courage for Papa to do this. And even though it appeared that he didn't think he did wrong by us, yet the fact that he agreed to such a meeting and carried through with it, convinced us that Papa did sincerely want to be forgiven.

I told my siblings, "I think I'll write a book called, "You don't have to be a crazy mixed up kid, even if you come from a dysfunctional family."

"Great idea," chimed in my sisters and brother. "You could show how we all survived and are all loyal to God and our churches."

"And you know," Andy said, "I never knew I came from a dysfunctional family until I was older. Life seemed normal to me."

"We owe a big thanks to Mama for that feeling, don't we?" I asked.

"Yes," said Nancy. "And you know what made a big difference? Mama was always there."

"Yes," everybody chimed in. "She was not only there, but she prayed for us. And God was with us through it all."

"Hey," responded Andy, "that could be the title for another book, 'Mother was always there!'"

CHAPTER 17

A year after the reconciliation meeting, Jenny died at the nursing home. Then Papa, in failing health and with some dementia, came to Lancaster County to live in a retirement home not far from Phil and me. Even there, he wanted to wear his suit and tie, but it was sad to see mashed potatoes smeared on the sleeves, and food spilled down the front of his shirt. We took some of his good suits away so we didn't have to keep getting them dry cleaned, and got him some wash and wear jackets. He had some nice sweaters, but he didn't like to wear them. Another thing he kept asking for, "Do you have a lozenger or something?" So we got in the habit of taking rolls of lifesavers along when we visited him. He had lots of nice shoes in the closet. But what do we see when we come to visit? His old white shoes!

The people at the nursing home liked Papa. By request, he led in prayer before meals. They also enjoyed his singing. His voice stood out in the group.

Several years before Papa moved to the nursing home, Mama's health was so fragile that we all felt she needed professional nursing care. Beth and Grandma sold the rancher house, had auction of Mother's things and moved to a Mennonite retirement community. Beth lived in a cottage, and Mama lived in skilled care. We children all visited Mama faithfully.

On at least one occasion Papa visited her there before he was in nursing care. One of Mama's regular nurses saw him, and got a big charge out of Mama saying, "Isn't he some dude?" The nurse related this to me later. I didn't really know what a "dude" was, so I looked it up in the dictionary. "A man fastidious in dress and manner," is what I learned. Mama had that right!

Later, when Mama didn't communicate well anymore, Papa said, "That's such a pity. She used to be the life of the party."

When we knew Mama was dying, I called Papa and asked if he had anything to say to Mama. "I don't know what to say," he said. "It just makes me very sad."

We four sisters arrived in time to be with Mama when she died at age 96.

At the funeral service in the Mennonite Church, the grandchildren sang a few of Mama's favorite songs. Andy's four sons did a marvelous rendition of "How Beautiful Heaven

Must Be." Here we realized that our parents' legacy of music is passed along to the next generations.

After the funeral, which Papa attended, he said, "She was a good woman. She was a good wife and a good mother." He repeated that over and over to different family members. It almost seemed that in his last years, and since Jenny's death, Papa's thoughts were back with Mama and the earlier years. *Could it be*, I wondered, *that a part of his life was wiped out from his memory?*

EPILOGUE

Five months after Mama died, I received a call from the nursing home where Papa lived. This time it was not Papa's strong voice I heard, but the soft voice of a nurse.

"May I speak with Amanda?"

"This is Amanda."

"Your father is near his end. If you want to see him alive, you will need to come soon. We don't think he'll make it through the night."

I quickly called my three sisters, my three half sisters, and my brother. Sarah didn't feel that she could get away from responsibilities at home just then, and Andy was too far away. Julie and her husband started on their way.

A few hours later, Nancy and Tom, Beth, Julie, and George, Phil and I, found Papa not responding. We stood around his bed, sang, prayed and spoke words of love and caring for him. It made us weary watching and listening to his labored breathing. Gradually, his breathing became shallow and he peacefully passed away.

When the nurse told us it was the end, I felt a great sense of relief and a light feeling. I can hardly explain it. I think it must have been from God.

Julie stood by the window weeping silently, and suddenly called, "Look. There's a rainbow!"

We all hurried to the window and stood in awe as we viewed the perfect arch, a beautiful rainbow with all the colors showing brightly.

Was the rainbow a sign of the faithfulness of God? Of His forgiveness? Of welcoming Papa home?

We, the children of both Mama and Jenny, cooperated in planning the funeral service at the Mennonite church where Papa attended as a child. We enjoyed a little humor along with these preparations. At the suggestion of one of Papa's nurses we put a roll of wintergreen lifesavers in his jacket pocket. "Do you have some lifesavers?" was his frequent request. We had him dressed in suit and tie, but under the cover we left him wear his favorite old worn white shoes.

We had lots of singing at the funeral, a solo by son, Andy, a quartet by four grandsons, and of course his favorite song, "My Jesus I Love Thee."

We bonded together well in this time of final goodbyes to Steve Johns, who was Papa for Mama's family, and Daddy for Jenny's family, and Grandpa to the next generation.

Papa's parting did not end the friendship between the two families. We continue to keep in touch and care about each other. Perhaps our friendship has become the silver lining to the clouds of sorrow and pain we each experienced.

ABOUT THE AUTHOR

MARTHA DENLINGER STAHL is a retired teacher living in a retirement community with her second husband, Clayton Nissley. Martha obtained her B.S. in El. Ed. from Eastern Mennonite College (Now EMU), and her Masters in Ed. from Millersville State Teacher's College (Now MU). She taught elementary school for twenty years. She and her first husband, Omar Stahl, spent time in Germany under Eastern Mennonite Missions. Presently she is active in Lyndon Mennonite Church.

She enjoys travel, reading, writing, water color painting, walking, playing pool with her husband, doing word puzzles, playing word games, and keeping up with friends on email.

Her previously published books are, Real People: Amish and Mennonites in Lancaster County, Pennsylvania; By Birth or By Choice: Who Can Become a Mennonite; Second Wife: Stories and Wisdom from Women Who Have Married Widowers.